LANDSCAPING
INDOORS
Bringing the Garden Inside

Scott D. Appell-Guest Editor

Janet Marinelli

SERIES EDITOR

Sigrun Wolff Saphire

ASSOCIATE EDITOR

Mark Tebbitt

SCIENCE EDITOR

Anne Garland

ART DIRECTOR

Steven Clemants

VICE-PRESIDENT SCIENCE & PUBLICATIONS

Judith D. Zuk

PRESIDENT

Elizabeth Scholtz

DIRECTOR EMERITUS

Handbook #165

Copyright © Winter 2000 by the Brooklyn Botanic Garden, Inc.

Handbooks in the *21st-Century Gardening Series,* formerly *Plants & Gardens,*
are published quarterly at 1000 Washington Ave., Brooklyn, NY 11225.

Subscription included in Brooklyn Botanic Garden subscriber membership dues ($35.00 per year).

ISSN # 0362-5850   ISBN # 1-889538-18-3

Printed by Science Press, a division of the Mack Printing Group.

Printed on recycled paper.

TABLE OF CONTENTS

LIVING WITH PLANTS

SCOTT D. APPELL

WE HAVE BECOME A NATION OF SAVVY GARDENERS, indeed! Over the past decades, devoted amateur horticulturists have successfully executed some remarkable gardening feats: we landscape and plant our own property, grow and force Belgian endive destined for our dining table, cultivate and utilize astounding arrays of edible and medicinal herbs, and we employ sophisticated plant propagation techniques—all outdoors.

But what about gardening indoors? What has happened to the ubiquitous houseplant? For the past forty years, successive generations of apartment dwellers and garden-less homeowners have had ample opportunity to get inspired by a multitude of gardening columns in the daily papers, an ever-growing supply of plant-related books and periodicals, as well as groundbreaking TV and radio programs. But there is still one major flaw: all along, houseplants have been relegated to the windowsill, or perhaps treated as botanical specimens that had to be cultivated beneath cumbersome, unattractive artificial lights.

A sad fate, in view of the fact that wonderfully challenging and unconventional ways to cultivate houseplants existed more than 150 years ago. Unfortunately, the techniques of the time have been all but forgotten, relinquished to the horticultural archives. One purpose of this handbook is to rekindle an interest in those wondrous, forgotten contraptions and Victorian esthetics—combined with modern sensibilities and budgets. It is possible to live surrounded by potted plants, creating a warm, temperate or tropical environment inside—without the luxury of a greenhouse or garden room!

Due to a lack of adequate natural ambient light, most homes will require artificial lighting to accommodate an indoor landscape away from

With the help of potted houseplants, this dining room has been transformed into a lush indoor landscape.

the windowsill. The products enabling this venture have evolved greatly within the past few decades, allowing us to remove houseplants from cramped windowsills, dispense with unsightly light hoods, and create pleasing interior designs using various methods of illumination. Modern indoor gardeners can choose from a greatly expanded repertoire of tropical or temperate plant material, and are able to rely on safe, chemical-free, biological pest control techniques.

Expand your mind and esthetics. Peruse this handbook, enlarge your houseplant collection—and grow along with it. You will never look at houseplants the same way again.

A HISTORY OF LANDSCAPING INDOORS

SCOTT D. APPELL

IN THE BEGINNING, THERE *WAS* LIGHT—but there was *no* glass. The trial and error task of mastering the art of glassmaking was, by far, the most important factor enabling the cultivation of plants indoors. Before people learned the secret of glassmaking, which entails fusing sand (silica) with soda (sodium oxide) and lime (calcium oxide), nature made glass in two different ways. When lightning strikes sand, the heat sometimes fuses the sand into long slender glass tubes called fulgurites—commonly referred to as petrified lightning. And the intense heat of volcanic eruption sometimes fuses rocks and sands into a glass called obsidian.

Historians do not know exactly when, where, or how people first learned to make glass, but it is generally believed that it was first manufactured sometime in the 3000s BC. Early glass manufacture was slow, and it required hard, hot work. Glass blowing or glass pressing were unknown and furnaces were small and lacked sufficient heat for proper melting. Glassmaking was such a costly enterprise that the ancient Egyptians relegated glass to jewelry making—achieving dazzling colors by adding metallic oxides to a basic recipe.

Starting in the 17th century, newly discovered flora arrived in Europe from all over the world aboard the trading vessels that crisscrossed the oceans. Orchids, pictured at left, palms, camellias, aroids, sansevierias, and cacti were among the many plants that found their way into European glasshouses.

CLIMATE CONTROL

The construction of artificial climates for plants is first alluded to in 500 BC Greece, in reference to the "Gardens of Adonis" (which were probably early precursors to cold frames). In his work *Phaedo(n)*, Plato remarks: *"A grain of seed, or the branch of a tree placed in or introduced to these gardens, acquired in eight days a development which cannot be obtained in as many months in the open air."*

In the first century AD, the Roman Columnella, who wrote about gardening and agriculture in his work *De Re Rustica* ("About All Things Rural"), describes the cultivation of cucumbers in large, covered containers (ingeniously piped with hot water). *"It is also possible, if it be worth the trouble, for wheels to be put on to the larger vessels so that they can be brought out with less labor. In any case, the vessels ought to be covered with slabs of transparent stone, so that in cold weather when the days are clear, they may be brought into the sun. By this method Tiberius Caesar was supplied with cucumbers during almost the whole year."*

The aforementioned "transparent stone" was *lapis specularis* (according to Pliny and Seneca), the complex silicate now commonly called mica. This mineral forms in thin, flexible, transparent or translucent layers, which are easily separated.

WINDOW PLANTING

By the 1870s the technology of growing plants indoors was evolving at breakneck speed, as people developed a frenzied interest in anything tropical. Indoor gardeners on both sides of the Atlantic witnessed the arrival of creatively designed horticultural home furnishings in vast quantities and myriad styles. The trend-setting paraphernalia of the time enabled gardeners to landscape their interiors, assuming there was sufficient ambient light.

It was in 50 AD that the first window glass was manufactured. This paved the way for the development of the greenhouse, glasshouse, and glazed windows for private residences during the next eight centuries. The enormous expense of manufacture made glass cost-prohibitive for most people, so glazed windows remained a luxury for the abodes of royalty, the homes of the landed gentry and wealthy merchants, and ecclesiastical buildings. Through most of history, the homes of the lower ranks were designed with small windows that either had little or no glass, relying on shutters that could be closed in inclement weather.

GLASS MANUFACTURE

In Europe in the early 1800s, there was a great demand for window glass, which was then called "crown glass." It was made by blowing a bubble of glass and spinning it until it was flat. This left a sheet of glass with a bump or "crown" in the center. The bump was removed, and the rest was cut into flat panes. A highly skilled craft, manufacturing crown glass required ten specialist glassmakers. By 1825 the "cylinder" process had replaced the crown method. In this technique, the molten glass was blown into the shape of a cylinder. After the cylinder cooled, it was sliced down one side. When reheated, the cylinder opened up to form a large sheet of thin clear

PLANT STAND

PLANTED CANDELABRA

window glass. Thanks to this process, larger, higher quality glazed windows were introduced—which were slapped with an incredibly steep tax based on the size of the window aperture. Consequently, in the homes of the majority of the population, windows remained small or were absent altogether. It wasn't until after 1890 that machinery was developed for precise, continuous manufacture of sheet glass and the glass tax was lifted in Europe, assuring glazed windows for everyone.

PEOPLE AND PLANTS

What, exactly, were the Romans growing in their *lapis specularis*-covered structures in addition to cucumbers? Historians don't know precisely which plants were cultivated, but they do concur that in all likelihood, they were destined for the dining table. Members of the well-heeled aristocracy of the Roman Empire were apparently very partial to tasty, out-of-season, and possibly aphrodisiacal vegetable tidbits. However, the Romans did force flowers for sheer pleasure, as this remark from Seneca indicates: "[Is it not] *contrary to nature to require a rose in winter and to use hot water to force from winter the later blooms of spring?*"

During the Crusades (1096–1291) a wide variety of hardy herbaceous and woody plants—including roses, tulips, and peonies—were brought back from the Middle East to be cultivated outdoors in European church gardens and royal landscapes. The landscape was devoid of greenhouses, and plants weren't cultivated indoors; the Age of Exploration was several centuries in the future.

Organized collections of plants destined for the *viridarium* (a heated wooden shed for overwintering plants) first appeared in the 14th century, most notably in Salerno and Venice. In the 16th century, they evolved into botanical gardens throughout Europe with the founding of the universities at Padua (1533), Pisa (1544), Bologna (1568), Leipzig (1580), Leyden (1587), and Paris (1597). It was not until the Renaissance that there was a methodical approach to the study of nature, and, in particular, the growth of plants.

IMPORTING PLANTS

Newly discovered flora arrived by the shipload in European glasshouses from all over the world, thanks, of course, to the vast fleets of trading vessels and the ever-elongating reach of commerce. European gardeners of the 17th through 19th centuries saw the arrival of orchids from the Philippines, palms from Madagascar, camellias from China, aroids from South America, sansevierias from South Africa, aspidistras from Japan, and cacti from North America. In the latter part of the 17th century, the first pineapple (also indigenous to South America) was grown to fruition in the greenhouses of Hampton Court Palace in London. By 1739, the brazier-heated greenhouses and glasshouses of the aristocracy were brimming with tropical plants, but ordinary people were still not growing plants in their homes.

It took another 120 years for the notion of growing tropical plants within the home to be legitimized as an engaging hobby, making the phenomenon a surprisingly recent occurrence. By the 1870s the technology of indoor horticulture was evolving at breakneck speed, as people developed a frenzied interest in anything tropical. Indoor

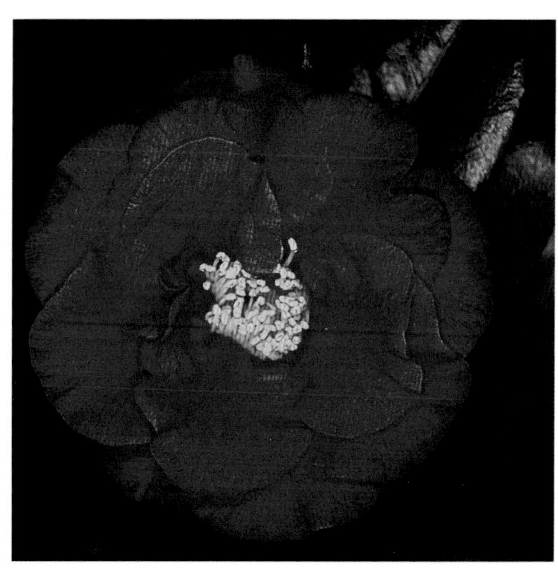

Camellias, native to China, became popular houseplants in Europe and America.

gardeners on both sides of the Atlantic witnessed the arrival of creatively designed horticultural home furnishings in vast quantities and myriad styles. Rolling planters, plant cabinets, indoor arches and trellises, Wardian cases, ornate pot brackets, attractive arborettes (designed specifically for ferns), and plantable ceiling chandeliers abounded in the front parlors of any family with "discriminating taste." The trend-setting paraphernalia of the time enabled horticulturists to landscape their interiors—assuming there was sufficient ambient light. It is no surprise that those plants that tolerated low light levels became immensely popular. Aspidistras, palms, rubber trees, sansevierias, aroids, English ivy, and ferns became a must for any parlor garden.

As a side effect, the number of horticultural products geared towards indoor gardeners became staggering—for the time. Water-spraying squeegees and syringes, as well as insecticide sprayers and hand-held fumigators, made their appearance. And the manufacturers of horticultural products answered the needful clamor of the new indoor gardening public by introducing the mail-order garden catalog.

People have remained fascinated with indoor gardening, and many of us are familiar with a succession of interesting fads: the "bromeliad tree" of the 1920s and '30s, the terrarium craze of the 1960s, and the macrame plant hangers of the 1970s. The houseplant hobby lagged for a decade or so but experienced a renaissance in the 1980s. And it shows no signs of slowing down as an ever-increasing number of people desire to bring the outdoors inside in new and innovative ways.

FOUR INDOOR GARDEN DESIGNS

BILL SHANK

IN THE MID-19TH CENTURY, A CRAZE for cultivating exotic plants indoors swept England. The Victorian home was more agreeable for plants than most modern living quarters because it was not overheated, but less agreeable because it was so dark. People filled their homes with freshly imported flora from all over the world, displaying their treasures in myriad inventive new ways. The plans I'm suggesting for creating intriguing indoor gardens are actually based on Victorian examples that are just as fresh and innovative today as they were a century and a half ago.

The indoor landscape can form an integral part of your interior and, naturally, reflect your personal preference and style. Do you want your landscape to be a strong focal point within the room, or perhaps be more subdued and neutral? How should you consider different leaf and flower colors? Plants with dark or light green, gray or variegated leaves tend to add a relaxed ambience to a room—philodendrons, variegated *Ficus* or *Polyscias*, *Podocarpus,* or *Cereus* are a few examples. Bold colors, such as red, yellow, and orange, provide dramatic effects and statements—furnished by crotons, caladiums, marantas, coleus, or bright-blossomed anthuriums, hibiscus, or orchids.

Whatever your preference, you need to provide a hospitable environment and establish a suitable space. Air circulation, room temperature, moisture, and ambient light sources must all be taken into account. Select plants that are slow growing and pruning-tolerant. Consider shrubs or large foliage plants if height is not a real issue. Use columnar-growing plants (such as *Afrocarpus falcata* or pole-trained vining aroids) for tall, narrow spaces and short, wide plants (*Philodendron bipinnatifidum* or *Ficus deltoidea*) for roomier quarters.

Think about layering plants in the fore-, middle-, and background. Have shorter plants grow at the bases of taller plants, as they would in nature. Avoid lining up plants in rows without regard for form, color, and foliage texture. You may want to switch flowering plants, such as orchids, into the indoor garden when they are in bloom and then move them to another location once their flowers are spent.

Think, too, about the containers you are going to use. They should blend with the color and style of your interior and shouldn't steal the show unless they are to be the focal point of the design.

ARMOIRE GARDEN

The idea of creating a miniature landscape in a piece of furniture dates back to Victorian times, as is witnessed by archival illustrations from the mid- to late 1800s, depicting lushly planted miniature oases. These ideal-

INDOOR LANDSCAPE: ARMOIRE

Using fans and artificial light, you can create a hospitable plant environment in a piece of furniture—an idea that dates back to Victorian times, as witnessed by the archival illustration at right.

ized visions of Victorian gardeners can actually become reality today with the right grow lamps to provide the necessary light and electric fans to keep the air circulating in a small enclosed space.

When converting an armoire into a plant cabinet, you need to protect it against humidity. Paint the interior walls with a light-reflecting, waterproof paint, or, better yet, line the walls with galvanized sheet metal panels, making sure that the seams are sealed with silicone aquarium glue. Make a two-inch sheet metal pan for the bottom of the cabinet and interior shelves to catch any water that drips from pots. Each pan should be filled with stones to keep the pots above the water level. The pans will help keep the plants in an environment of raised humidity.

Mount fluorescent lamps in the top of the cabinet and underneath any interior shelves, alternating between warm and cool white light bulbs or tubes in each section. Attach a board to the front of any interior shelves to hide the light fixtures from view. Use fluorescent lamps in a small cabinet because they emit less heat and are thinner than incandescent bulbs.

If the doors have glass panels, they can be shut to further increase the humidity. A small fan should be installed above each group of plants to move the air and avoid the growth of fungus.

WINDOW GARDEN

The usual place for houseplants is the windowsill. Often it is too small for the number of plants collected by the true plantoholic and does not provide enough light for the plants you want to grow.

Taking an idea from a Victorian illustration, the inventive gardener can increase the window space by building a glass-enclosed "window box" that juts out into the room. Use lumber to build a structural frame and fit it with ¼-inch thick glass panels on the top, one side, and the front. Fit the second side with a glazed door that allows access to the plants and can be opened to regulate the buildup of heat and humidity. Line the bottom and the sides of the box to two inches with galvanized sheet metal and fill this "pan" with a one-inch layer of stones. Plants can be set on the base or mounted on brackets attached to the sides of the window frame. Cast iron gas-lamp brackets are an attractive option. They can often be found in antique stores.

If the window receives full sun, choose plants that are sun-tolerant, and/or control the intensity of the light that reaches sensitive plants. Either mount a fabric sunscreen or position pots of tender plants in the shade of larger sun-tolerant plants.

If the window doesn't get enough sun, you'll need to install additional lighting. Your options are fluorescent lamps in industrial fixtures, such as those sold for home workshops, or grow bulbs, which may be screwed into a China-cap hanging fixture (as in the illustration on opposite page).

INDOOR LANDSCAPE: WINDOW

Taking an idea from a Victorian illustration, the inventive gardener can increase window growing space by building a glass-enclosed "window box" that juts out into the room. If the window doesn't get enough sun, you may have to install additional lighting, as shown at left.

INDOOR LANDSCAPE DESIGN

CLOSET GARDEN

The Victorians created garden rooms in their homes, but were limited in their plant choices by the amount of available natural light. Some old illustrations seem to be overly optimistic in terms of the plantings they suggest, but with the addition of artificial lights, they are easily implemented today, even if there is no natural light available in the space.

How about transforming a walk-in closet into a garden? The first step is to replace the solid closet doors with glass French doors. If the ceiling is high, consider a raised platform to separate the garden from the rest of the room. The space below the platform is an excellent place to install a sunken water feature, and it allows you to hide the plant containers below the "garden floor" (see the illustration on page 16).

INDOOR LANDSCAPE: CLOSET

How about transforming a walk-in closet into a garden? The one shown above has an Asian theme that is further explored in the choice of containers. A bamboo grid is attached to the back wall and an Asian wall hanging is displayed to expand the theme. A Victorian design is shown at left.

If the ceiling is too low to allow for a raised platform, or if it is impractical for the site, set the pond and the plants in their trays onto the floor and camouflage with artificial or real stones, and smaller plants. Don't forget to check the weight limit of your floor and stay within the load limit.

Make sure to line any sunken areas and/or the surface of the floor with a waterproof rubber pool liner to catch any escaped water that could cause damage to the building structure. The sunken pool can be a fiberglass pond from a garden center mounted one inch above the floor surface. Make sure it is installed perfectly level so it does not leak into the liner below.

Set the sunken pots on stone-filled trays on the bottom liner. Be extremely careful when watering to prevent water from collecting under the plants. Remove the plants from their holes periodically and check for water accumulation. If you find water, dab it up with a large sponge.

As a finishing touch, you may want to hide the pot edges and the pool liner with pebbles. Light the garden with high intensity discharge (HID) lamps and include a fan in the design to circulate the air.

GARDEN ROOM

The most ambitious and rewarding project is to create a whole room that is dedicated to gardening. If the space has windows, they can provide for air circulation and some minimal light. You will have to install additional lighting though, as most plants are going to be too far away from the windows. Work with a combination of timer-controlled HID and incandescent grow lights to give the plants the amount of light they need. Fans help circulate the air.

The walls should be painted a light-reflecting color and may be decorated with architectural elements for an outdoor ambience. The floor should have a durable and waterproof cover to avoid damage from leaking pots and dripping hoses. A relatively inexpensive way to do this is to lay down a heavy-duty pool liner and cover it with loose-laid bricks or tiles, creating an indoor terrace. (Remember to check the weight load for your structure and do not exceed the limit, allowing for floor covering and plants.) Japanese *shoji* sliding panels, for example, create the feeling of an exterior window wall and separate the room from the interior space.

Group plants by size, color, texture, and form, bearing light and water requirements in mind. Place the plants in decorative pots. Custom-built wooden planters with adjustable shelving allow you to raise plants to the level you desire. In that way shorter plants can gain height and become tall enough for you to sit under. Use smaller plants to hide large containers to give the appearance of a planted landscape.

For easier maintenance, grow smaller plants in individual pots that can be moved to the bath tub or kitchen sink for a good showering. Large plants have to be cleaned in place. Close access to water is recommended. Alternatively, you may want to use a small-gauge hose, available in custom sizes up to 75 feet, that can be attached to a faucet by a removable clip-on feature.

INDOOR LANDSCAPE: GARDEN ROOM

The most ambitious and rewarding project: creating a whole room dedicated to gardening. The design above achieves an outdoor ambience for an indoor terrace. At right, a 19th century example of a garden room.

If you are planning to use the room at night, consider installing some low-wattage light fixtures, such as outdoor garden lights, to create a pleasant atmosphere, as plant lights seem very strong and harsh at night. A focal point—for example a sculptural form, or even a splashing wall fountain—can finish the outdoor feel of the room. Small flowering plants and cut flowers complete the illusion of a country garden room.

INDOOR LANDSCAPE DESIGN

WARDIAN CASES AND TERRARIUMS

SCOTT D. APPELL

FOR THE BUSY INDOOR GARDENERS who may not have the time to continually check house plants for water or humidity levels, or for the inhabitants of arid, dusty, infernally-heated homes, growing plants within enclosed glass containers is a beautiful, viable landscape option. Most of us know these glass boxes as terrariums, and in fact, indoor gardeners have relied upon their virtues since the 1850s, when they held the place of honor in every respectable parlor garden.

HISTORY

The humble terrarium has truly remarkable beginnings. In the early 19th century, Britain was already in the throes of the Industrial Revolution. At the time, there were no rules pertaining to the release of industrial wastes, and in industrialized areas everywhere, the landscape was void of flora and fauna, killed off by the soot, the smoke, and the polluted water. The human inhabitants of this bleak world were not faring any better, suffering and dying from pollution-related ailments.

In the summer of 1829, the physician Nathaniel B. Ward, a general practitioner who diagnosed and treated many patients with pollution-induced pulmonary ailments, noticed that the herbaceous plants in his factory-surrounded, smoke-inundated garden were dying in spite of all his best horticultural efforts. He was greatly upset by this course of events, but his mind was preoccupied with an entomological experiment he was performing. He had buried the pupa of a common sphinx moth within a small pile of compost inside a wide-mouthed glass bottle covered with a lid and placed the container on a sunny windowsill. He observed

WARDIAN CASE

A closed glass container makes an excellent environment for plants, as the English physician Nathaniel B. Ward discovered accidentally while experimenting with sphinx moths in 1829. The ornate "Wardian case" at left and the modern variation shown at right are two interpretations of his groundbreaking discovery. Wardian cases were also used to hold tropical plants during their long sea voyages from their countries of origin to England.

that the moisture, which during the heat of the day arose from the compost, condensed on the interior surface of the glass, and trickled back down into the compost, thus keeping the internal environment at a constant level of moisture and humidity. Shortly before the insect emerged as an adult, Ward noticed a tiny volunteer fern (*Dryopteris filix-mas*) and grass (*Poa annua*) sprouting. What immediately struck him was the luxuriance with which the tender fern was growing—he had never been able to cultivate ferns in the garden or on his windowsill. It was quickly evident to him that the plants were able to obtain light, heat, moisture, and humidity inside the bottle just as well as outside of it—with the added bonus that the lid, which retained the moisture, excluded the soot and smoke. (He quickly forgot his experiment with the sphinx moth.)

The physician became mesmerized with the implications of this new way of cultivating flora. He began to experiment wildly and widely with plants grown within glass containers, which became known as "Wardian cases." There were variable degrees of success, of course, but some plants did extremely well.

For indoor gardeners, the Wardian case came to play a very important role in two ways. It became the means by which tropical plants could be successfully conveyed to England from their distant countries of origin. Prior to this new shipping technique, shiploads of newly discovered and collected plant material often dried up, withered away from lack of humidity, or succumbed to salt spray or cold while in transit.

And at the same time that plant collectors and botanists were utilizing Ward's innovation, indoor gardeners were introducing terrariums with great verve into their homes. Beginning with the lidded glass bottle, their designs became more and more elaborate as the fashion took hold. Some

Wardian cases were devised as huge pieces of elaborately carved, ornamental cabinetry constructed from choice woods such as oak, mahogany, and rosewood. Some looked like miniature greenhouses. Another style featured a custom-made cylindrical dome. Other forms were more modest, covered rectangular boxes of glass, sometimes sitting on fashionable legs. All in all, the use of hand-made glass made the cases extremely expensive, but any household with enough disposable income made sure to have one. Nature indoors became the rage.

BUILDING A WARDIAN CASE

Once again, growing plants in enclosed glass containers is in vogue, and the modern-day horticulturist can emulate the trends of the Victorians in several ways. One possibility is to purchase a fabulous antique Wardian case dating to the 1860s for several thousand dollars. Or you can buy a piece of vintage or new furniture, and redesign it into a Wardian case. For example, a glass aquarium can be affixed to a piano bench with aquarium silicone sealant. The unattractive juncture can be covered up with strips of wood stained the same color as the bench. Cover the top with a store-bought glass cover, or have one custom-made. The result is a Victorian-style rolling Wardian case.

For a more ambitious project, obtain an old breakfront or a similar piece that has glass fronts. Refinish the exterior wood if necessary and remove the various internal shelves and hardware. The idea is to build a waterproof box inside the cabinet. Carefully measure the inside dimensions, and have mirrors custom-cut to fit inside the cabinet; the mirrors reflect light and thus aid plant growth. The mirrors should fit snugly on the bottom, the two sides, and the back. A two-inch strip of clear glass should be installed in the front to provide a lip that will contain any water build-up. If the sides of the piece are glass, use clear glass for the side "lips" as well. Leave about eight inches from the top for the installation of lights and fans for air circulation. In order to protect the cabinet from moisture, seal all the glass pieces with silicone aquarium glue.

Install fluorescent lamps at the top of the cabinet, alternating between cool and warm white tubes, and hook them up to a timer. Mount one or two small electric fans, depending on the size of the case. A fan is crucial when cultivating such epiphytes as orchids and bromeliads.

Industrious indoor landscapers can even make their own enclosed glass containers using flat glass panes and silica gel. By cutting the glass to specific sizes and shapes, and bonding the glass with a water-tight seal, you can create any number of designs.

If all this sounds like too much trouble, you can buy a beautiful Victorian-inspired Wardian case for a reasonable price or transform any attractive glass jar into a plant environment.

TOOLS OF THE TRADE

Due to the unusual shapes and openings of terrariums and Wardian cases, specialized planting and cultural tools are required. They are based on the standard tools for outdoor gardening, but modified for the job: they need to be thinner, smaller, and have longer handles than their conventional counterparts. With a little imagination, all of them can be made at home. For example: small forks and slender spoons can be affixed to lengths of bamboo stakes to become miniature long-handled shovels or rakes. Corks, large buttons, or rubber stoppers, attached to bamboo "handles," become long-reaching soil stompers and tappers. Long handles allow safety razors or craft (X-acto) knife blades to become pruners or machetes. On the end of a long chopstick, a soft artist's brush becomes a broom that gently removes soil or debris from tender foliage, and a stake-mounted carpet or crafting needle becomes a trash-removal spike. Tiny sponges convert to miniature window cleaners to wash the interior surface of the glass. Kitchen funnels flawlessly dispense soil into slender-necked or narrow-mouthed bottles and jars. In addition, long tongs or spring-release grippers from the aquarium supply store are perfect for lowering plants through narrow openings or into especially deep cases. A hand-held spray bottle or atomizer makes a handy washing, humidifying, or watering device.

PLANTS FOR WARDIAN CASES

Create the garden of your choice in an enclosed glass container. Gloxinias (*Sinningia*) (**A**, top left) can be used for a temperate garden. Episcias (**B**, top right) and orchids (**C**, above left) can be part of a tropical environment, and opuntias (**D**, above right) are suitable for a desert garden.

PLANTING

As with all landscape projects, begin from the ground up. Before scooping or funneling a layer of soil into the container, lay down a layer of drainage material. I prefer natural-looking pea gravel, and include a two- to three-inch layer, depending on the size of the container. You can hide the gravel from view by covering it with soil towards the outside of the terrarium.

The Wardian case can be filled with as much soil as needed for the plants you pick; from one to six inches is typical. Feel free to manipulate the soil into any topographic feature you desire. Water-tight containers placed in the miniature landscape can simulate pools or ponds, with flat pebbles, slate, or river stones camouflaging the edges.

Practically any type of plant can be cultured in an enclosed glass container. Try your favorite tropical houseplants that cannot ordinarily be grown successfully on a windowsill. Create a tropical paradise with maidenhair ferns, episcias, creeping figs, anthuriums, columneas, African violets, or pelleas. Design a desert garden using cacti and succulents. Stapelias, heurnias, opuntias, mammillarias, aloes, haworthias, and lithops are interesting choices, but bear in mind that this particular group of plants needs especially high light levels. Tropical forest canopies can be created within tall cases with the help of logs or small branches planted with epiphytes such as orchids, bromeliads, hoyas, aroids, or gesneriads (see "The Epiphyte Tree," page 25). Cold, sunny rooms can harbor glass cases containing miniature gardens planted with myrtles, malpighias, small-leafed citrus, *Ficus*, dwarf pomegranates and pygmy bamboo.

Plant your selections using the battalion of specialized tools you have constructed, making sure to gently firm the soil around the plants. Decorate the mini-environment with your favorite natural finds: rocks, stones, living, pre-soaked sheet moss, driftwood, or bark fragments. Remember that collecting forest moss or Spanish moss from the wild is illegal. However, florist supply houses usually carry both materials.

WATERING AND PRUNING

Freshly planted specimens must be watered in. Using room-temperature water dispensed through a watering can with a narrow opening, gently saturate the soil. Keep in mind that you can easily deliver too much water—which is impossible to drain off and will invariably drown the plants. Water slowly—allowing the soil to absorb the moisture. Mist the foliage as well, and affix the cover. Check moisture levels daily and add more water as necessary. If the case is illuminated with artificial lights, it needs to be watered and misted frequently. Cactus- and succulent-filled desert environments must not be watered at all for the first few weeks.

Administer your favorite brand of water-soluble fertilizer monthly. Never add it to dry soils—the plant roots may be irreparably damaged. Moisten the earth prior to fertilizing. Foliar feeding is beneficial as well. A successful planting will grow luxuriantly, filling out the entire space. Don't be afraid of ruthless pruning—the plants will appreciate it. If some of the plants appear to grow poorly, don't hesitate to remove them and replace them with another choice. Your hard work will reward you with years of pleasure.

THE EPIPHYTE TREE

ELLEN ZACHOS

BEHOLD THE LOVELY EPIPHYTE TREE. Each is unique. You won't find one at your local garden center or in your favorite mail-order catalog. So, where can you locate one of these delicate and desirable beauties? Roll up your sleeves and get out a drop cloth, because you're going to make it yourself!

Epiphytes are plants that, in their natural habitats, grow on trees. Many are understory plants of the rainforest that do not require direct sunlight. Their thick leaves and heavy epidermis allow them to survive without direct contact to groundwater supplies. Specially developed roots are used for anchorage and absorb water and nutrients from the surrounding humid air. Many epiphytes also have "pseudobulbs," or fleshy roots that store water for times of drought. Epiphytes are not parasitic and take no nutrients from their hosts. They get some nutrients from debris that falls down through the canopy, into the crotches of trees or the indents in cliff surfaces where they thrive.

While many epiphytes can

A branch planted with epiphytes.

adapt to life in a pot, they do not require soil like most other houseplants. They can easily be mounted on logs or branches to mimic the way they grow in nature. If you have a passion for exotic tropical plants, an epiphyte tree is your chance to create a thing of rare beauty. But beware: this project is not for the faint of heart. The finished product requires substantially more maintenance than potted plants, and the bigger the tree, the more complicated the maintenance.

PLANTS FOR THE EPIPHYTE TREE

Bromeliads are probably the most familiar epiphytes. They grow perched in the most unassuming roadside trees and shrubs in the more tropical parts of the U.S. and range in size from one-inch-tall tillandsias to vriesea species with bloom spikes that grow to three feet. The Bromeliad family is widely variable, with many species well suited to life on a man-made tree, including members of the *Neoregelia, Aechmea, Vriesea, Guzmania,* and *Tillandsia* genera.

Let's look at some of the tougher epiphytes, plants that will thrive, take root, and prosper in a home environment. Many orchids are epiphytes, including the sturdy and easy-to-find *Phalaenopsis. Vanda* and *Ascocentrum* species are also epiphytic, although they are more demanding, with higher humidity requirements than most people can meet in their homes. The genus *Hoya* includes over 200 species, many of which are epiphytic and well suited to the task at hand. Epiphytic ferns like staghorn (*Platycerium bifurcatum*) and rabbit's foot (*Davallia fejeensis*) are also excellent choices. *Rhipsalis* species, holiday cactus (*Schlumbergera* species), and orchid cactus (*Epiphyllum* species) are also interesting, with many providing showy blooms and berries at different times of the year.

Remember not to go overboard when choosing your plants. It's enormously tempting to assemble a wide assortment of showy plants, but take some time to really consider your end result. Your tree will look better if you limit yourself to four to six different types of plants, perhaps even fewer depending on the size of your project. You don't want the plants competing with each other for attention; they should work together as a cohesive whole. While splashy and exotic flower colors are wonderful, make sure to choose colors that work together.

CHOOSING A BRANCH

The first step is to choose a branch or log, so take a walk in the woods or your local park. (If you go browsing on public property, make sure to take only a downed, dead branch.) You should have an idea of where you want to put your finished epiphyte tree, so you can pick a branch of the appropriate size. Look for one with an interesting shape, and perhaps some nooks and crannies where you can tuck the occasional mini-specimen. A five-foot-tall piece of wood with a diameter of approximately three inches makes an excellent tree. When you get your branch back to the house, look at it from every angle. Trim any unwanted branches with pruners or a saw. If your branch is dirty or covered with lichen, scrub it with a 10 percent bleach solution and let it dry.

TO HANG OR TO STAND

Decide whether you want your tree to be free-standing or hanging. Each has several advantages: a hanging branch is more unusual and looks particularly dramatic across a large window or wall. To hang the branch, screw stainless steel eyes into the back and top and suspend it directly from hooks screwed into the window frame or use a thin cable. Be sure to consider the weight of the branch when you pick hooks, eyes and cable. A free-standing tree can easily be moved from place to place, should you want to rearrange your interior landscape, and it may be easier to assemble, since you can approach it from all angles.

BUILDING A BASE

A clay pot makes a nice base for a free-standing design. The weight of the pot helps keep the branch upright, and the color of the terra cotta should blend well with any other potted plants. Position the branch in the pot and add stones around its base for additional ballast. Make sure that the pot's drainage hole is covered, and, wearing gloves, pour Quikrete concrete or plaster of Paris into the pot, firming it in around the base of the branch. Either of these materials will be dry to the touch in 30 minutes, but let it harden overnight before you continue. (While plaster of Paris may weaken after several years of exposure to water, it is easier to work with and easier to find in small quantities.)

GETTING READY FOR ACTION

While the plaster dries, make some sketches of possible plant arrangements. The more time you spend on this, the less time you'll waste fumbling with plant material when it is most vulnerable, with its roots exposed to the drying air. When you are happy with your composition, assemble the rest of your tools.

A drop cloth is a must for easy cleanup, and if it is water-absorbent,

WHAT YOU'LL NEED

Branch
Terra cotta pot
Ballast stones
Plaster of Paris or Quikrete
Drop cloth
Epiphytic plants
Long-grain sphagnum moss
Fishing line or thin gauge wire
Hot glue gun (multi-temperature or low heat)
Glue sticks

PLANTING AN EPIPHYTE TREE

To add a plant to the epiphyte tree, remove it from its container and shake off as much potting mix as possible (**A**, left). Wrap the root in moss and tie the moss/root bundle to the tree with fishing line or wire (**B**, near right). Once you've arranged the larger plants on your branch, fill in some gaps with tillandsias. Since they don't have a root system, it's easiest to attach them with glue (**C**, right).

it will keep spills from spreading. You will also need sphagnum moss, transparent fishing line or thin-gauge wire, a glue gun with a low temperature setting, and glue sticks. You are going to attach most of the plants with fishing line or wire and sphagnum moss. Remove the first plant from its pot, shaking off as much potting mix as possible. Don't be afraid to comb through the roots with your fingers—these plants can take a little man-handling. Wrap the root system in moss and tie the moss/root bundle to the tree. Wire may be easier to work with, but I prefer fishing line because it is virtually invisible. If your branch has small side branches, you may be able to tuck the moss/root bundle into a natural niche without any tying whatsoever. After about six months, you should be able to remove the wire or line, as the plants' roots attach themselves to the branch.

PLANTING

Choose the focal point of your tree and start working outward from there. I suggest beginning with the larger, showier plants and using smaller specimens to fill in gaps and link one distinct visual area of the tree to another. Hoyas, for example, make excellent transition plants because their foliage lies close to the surface of the branch, like a groundcover. They will also flower several times a year, and many species are quite fragrant. When attaching a vining epiphyte to the tree, twine its stem around the branch. With time and humidity, the vine will develop epiphytic roots, which attach themselves to the tree.

Pause frequently as you work to look at your epiphyte tree from every angle. Do not overplant, or your tree will be a hodgepodge of mismatched specimens. As a finishing touch, fill in some small gaps with little tillandsias.

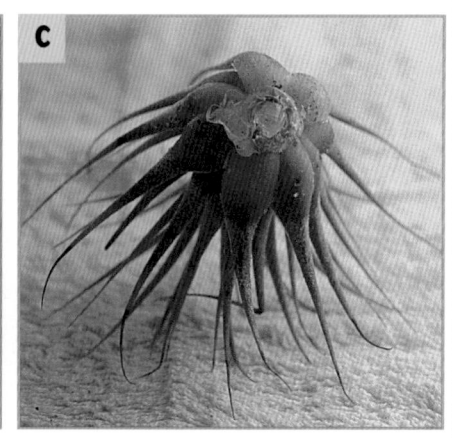

Since they don't have root systems like phalaenopsis, hoyas, and some other bromeliads, it's easiest to attach tillandsias with glue. Be sure to use the glue gun at a low setting, so as not to damage the plant tissue.

TREE MAINTENANCE

Congratulations, your tree is planted. Now let's talk maintenance. Because the plants are not growing in soil, which retains water and nutrients, they require more frequent attention. Obviously, they can't be watered in the traditional manner, so you'll have to consider an alternate method of watering or misting. Epiphytic logs or branches can be brought into the shower for a weekly soaking. A free-standing epiphyte tree can stand under the shower, and smaller branches can soak in a full tub. If you have a large hanging branch, you may want to install hooks in the ceiling of your shower. Suspending the branch will make watering considerably easier and will allow the branch to drip dry before it is replaced in the landscape. Don't forget to fill the center cups of all bromeliads after returning the tree to its place. If your planting is too heavy to be moved easily, it may be thoroughly misted or soaked in place. Use a two- to three-gallon pump sprayer containing water or a mixture of water and fertilizer.

In an emergency, you can get your epiphyte tree through a one-week absence, although I wouldn't advise doing this regularly. Bring your tree into the shower and open the faucet so that the smallest possible trickle of lukewarm water drips to the floor. (Make sure the drain is open.) Close the shower curtain and reduce the light to a minimum. With little light, the plants need less water and make do with the humidity produced by the dripping shower.

WATER GARDENING INDOORS

AN OASIS AGAINST THE ODDS

SCOTT D. APPELL

THE SOUND AND FEEL OF RUNNING WATER, the sight of flashing and darting fish, the smell of fragrant flowering aquatic flora, and even the taste of edible, home-grown water plants satisfies all of our senses. A water garden is a soothing, beautiful addition to the indoor landscape, and it does not have to be a financial burden.

CONTAINER CHOICE

Any non-porous container that can hold water—from the ridiculous to the sublime—can become an indoor water garden. Consider glass fish bowls or tanks, pre-formed ponds or pools, and thrift shop finds such as glazed watertight ceramic bowls and clear glass apothecary jars. Even such mundane kitchen equipment as glass cookware can be transformed into handsome water gardens. Simply cover the exterior with a layer of homemade "hypertufa." Mix two parts Quikrete concrete, three parts vermiculite, and three parts chopped sphagnum moss with enough water to moisten. Lather the outside of the container with a one- to two-inch-thick layer and let it dry overnight.

Opposite: A water garden makes a spectacular addition to the indoor landscape.

BASIC BIOLOGY OF AQUATIC PLANTS

Aquatic plants are grouped into three categories based on the way they grow—emergent plants, submergent plants, and floaters. Emergent plants are rooted in the ground and produce foliage that remains at or above the surface of the water; these include cyperus (*Cyperus* species), arrowhead (*Sagittaria* species), and water snowflake (*Nymphoides* species). Submergent plants, which are also firmly rooted in the soil, have leaves that remain below the surface of the water; they include elodea (*Elodea canadensis*) and eelgrass (*Vallisneria americana*). The third category, floaters, includes plants that freely float on the open surface of the water—though they may have been rooted in the soil as seedlings. This group includes duckweeds (*Lemna* species and *Wolffia* species), water chestnuts (*Trapa* species) and water lettuce (*Pistia stratiotes*).

To make matters more complex, aquatic plants are divided into warm- and cold-water plants. The water plants indigenous to the warm waters of tropical South America, Africa, and Asia—such as the sword plants (*Echinodorus* species), *Cryptocoryne* species and water ferns (*Ceratopteris* species)—require permanent warmth, provided by an aquarium heater, for example.

VICTORIAN PARLOR AQUARIUM

Cold-water submergent and emergent aquatics, which are indigenous to North America, Northern Europe, and temperate Asia—such as parrot feather (*Myriophyllum* species), *Aponogeton* species and calamus (*Acorus* species)—do well in an unheated pool, provided that the water temperature never dips below 50° F.

SOIL REQUIREMENTS

In nature, aquatic plants live in the nutrient-rich substrate of naturally occurring streams, ponds, pools, marshes, and fens. The soils are extremely high in organic matter, and the various species grow luxuriantly. However, these biotic mires are unfit for indoor use—their nutrient levels are so high that a natural equilibrium is hard to obtain in a contained indoor setting. The result is often a methane-rich, smelly, sludgy mess. Therefore, it is necessary to culture water plants in a more stable and less obtrusive (thus less fertile) substrate, relying on chemical fertilizers for nutrients.

A soil recipe that works well for containerized emergent plants is one part soil to three parts builder's or aquarium sand. It's a good idea to wash the sand in a sieve until the water runs clear before use. A "mulch" layer of fine-grade aquarium gravel also helps prevent the soil from clouding the water. This recipe works for all sizes of emergent plants, such as taro (*Colocasia* species), papyrus (*Cyperus papyrus*), water maranta (*Thalia dealbata*), horsetail (*Equisetum hyemale*), or Chinese water chestnut (*Eleocharis dulcis*).

For clear glass aquarium-style containers that are planted directly, or for small potted submergent plants, I use a mixture of equal parts coarse, sharp sand and pre-washed, natural, fine-grade aquarium gravel, with a little horticultural charcoal added for good measure. The charcoal is buoyant, so a post-planting layer of gravel is needed to avoid floating black bits.

For tank- or bowl-style water gardens, put down a layer of substrate that is appropriate for the dimensions of the container, for example about two to three inches for a 20-gallon aquarium and about six inches for a 60-gallon tank. You can grow aquatic plants in any size container in any soil depth—simply cultivate the appropriate kinds. Slopes, valleys, or other topographic features can be fashioned as desired and held in place with flat river stones, sheets of shale, or lakeside driftwood (it's difficult to boil out all of the salts from seaside finds). Avoid using limestone or sea shells, which will change the pH level of the water.

By the last quarter of the 19th century, indoor gardeners had begun incorporating aquariums into their parlor gardens. The ingenious footed water garden at left contrives to present its plant and fish life at eye level for convenient viewing.

WATER

To avoid disturbing the planting medium, fill the container slowly. Deflect the stream of water against the glass, a stone or your hand. To remove chlorine and fluoride, use a water conditioner from the aquarium store, a water purifier, or simply let the water stand, uncovered, for 24 hours.

Never use cold water to fill up your water garden, as it will shock the tropical plants. For a small tank, gently warm the water in a non-reactive stockpot. A large pool should be filled a week or so before planting to allow the water to reach room temperature, unless it is artificially heated.

PLANTING TECHNIQUES

There are two methods of cultivating plants in water. One is to install the plants directly in a growing medium spread on the bottom of a glass receptacle—as in the typical tropical aquarium. This technique looks best in clear glass containers. Remember that red- or blue-tinted or colored glass will filter out the light colors necessary for proper plant growth.

An alternate procedure involves placing the plants into individual pots or crates, and submerging these in the garden. This strategy works well with pre-fabricated polyethylene or fiberglass pools, ponds, and tubs.

As with any transplanting task, correct plant depth is crucial. Crown-forming submergent plants such as *Echinodorus, Cryptocoryne,* or *Barclaya* must not be planted too deeply—which means that you should plant them a little too shallowly, taking into account the final layer of gravel, which brings the substrate to the appropriate height. Branching or "stem-type" submergent plants, such as *Anacharis, Hygrophila,* and *Ludwigia* are usually sold as bunches of unrooted terminal shoots. They can be planted directly into the substrate, after removing the bottom foliage. Use a rock or stone to weight them down until they are rooted. Submergent floaters, such as *Ceratopteris* or *Nymphoides,* may simply be "released" and left to their devices; they will root as they grow. Emergent floaters such as *Azolla, Salvinia* or *Lemna,* may be treated in the same way.

LIGHTING

One of the most critical keys to success with indoor water gardens is light—both quality and quantity. You need to provide between twelve and sixteen hours of light a day. Some standard aquariums are fitted with light hoods. The covers come with a choice of 25-watt incandescent bulbs or 20-watt Vita-Lite fluorescent tubes. The incandescent bulbs create enough heat to warm the water (in small tanks), but will burn the foliage of emergent plants. The Vita-Lites are cool, creating no extraneous heat, and will not burn the foliage.

PLANTS FOR THE INDOOR WATER GARDEN

If you want to grow sun lovers like *Nymphoides indica*, water snowflake, (**A**, top left) or *Nymphea* 'Albert Greenberg', a tropical water-lily hybrid (**B**, top right), you need to provide plenty of light. If you don't want to install a lot of artificial lighting, take advantage of aquatic plants suited for shady situations, such as *Marsilea quadrifolia*, water clover (**C**, above left), and *Sagittaria*, arrowhead, (**D**, above right). And bear in mind that any non-porous container that can hold water may become an indoor water garden.

Larger gardens need larger lighting apparatus. Suspend a China-cap style lamp shade fitted with a 160-watt Gro-lux incandescent bulb 24 inches above a tub garden or a large bowl planting. Floor ponds and pools need special attention. Low-hanging fixtures will work, of course, but will block the view of the garden and look foolish. One or more ceiling-mounted 400-watt HID lamps will work well, but even these may not provide enough light for water-lilies (*Nymphaea* species) and lotus (*Nelumbo* species).

If you don't want to rig up a lot of artificial light, take advantage of aquatic plants suited for shady situations. Consider planting arrowheads (*Sagittaria*), calamus (*Acorus*), *Aponogeton*, elodea (*Elodea*), water clover (*Marsilea*), or quillwort (*Isoetes*), for example.

If you prefer to think small, try placing a water garden on a windowsill that gets morning sun. Or how about a wine glass or turtle bowl cultured under a desktop goose-neck lamp with a circular fluorescent bulb?

THE QUESTION OF ALGAE

Newly planted water gardens are susceptible to blooms of algae. This is a normal occurrence. As the algae become overpopulated, they eventually die off, and the water becomes permanently clear. Do not remove the green water and replace it with fresh—this will not allow for the natural "bell curve" of algae growth and death. Reducing the amount of light (if possible) will discourage algae growth. Freshwater snails will eat the algae from container walls and leaf surfaces. However, if there are too many snails, they may clog up filters and pumps. Avoid using wild, pond-caught snails. Never use a commercial algicide—one careless application will destroy all of the plants.

GENERAL CARE

Indoor water gardens need the same care as their exterior equivalents. Dead foliage must be removed weekly. Overgrown floaters must be thinned out so that the ambient light reaches the underplantings. Water evaporates quickly indoors, making it necessary to top off with additional water occasionally. A regular regimen of fertilizing is crucial for success. Aquatic plant food is sold in pellets that can be directly inserted into the soil every month. For large fish-free pools, mosquitoes may be a problem. Try using mosquito dunks that contain the bacterium *Bacillus thuringiensis* var. *israelensis*, which is deadly to mosquito larvae, but harmless to humans, pets, plants, and fish. Another useful product, Pond Saver, is a concentrated blend of beneficial bacteria which quickly biodegrade the organic matter in water that causes clouding, sludge, and foul odors. It is not harmful to fish or plants.

PALMS IN THE PARLOR

TOM McCLENDON

O F ALL THE MEMBERS OF THE PLANT KINGDOM suitable for use as houseplants, none evoke a feeling of the tropics like the palms. With their large, architectural leaves and strong outlines, palms can help create an indoor Garden of Eden wherever you live.

During the Victorian Era, indoor palms were all the rage in England, the U.S., and other countries. No house was complete without at least one kentia palm, *Howea forsteriana*. Since then the popularity of palms has waxed and waned—and waxed again; today it is rare to enter a restaurant or shopping mall without seeing at least a few palms, even if they're not always tastefully arranged. Fortunately, there is a wide selection of palms that can be grown successfully indoors.

Howea forsteriana, kentia palm.

Livistona chinensis, the Chinese fan palm, needs good light and water. This palm tends to spread out before growing up.

GROWING PALMS

Apartments and houses can be very inhospitable environments to most plants. Many people prefer a very dry indoor climate—with winter humidity levels that are lower than those of the Sahara Desert! To the degree that you can, try to make your home friendly to palms. In general, this means keeping things as bright and moist as you can.

If you have no real desire to recreate a tropical rainforest in your apartment, you're still in luck. Many of the palms suitable as houseplants are native to tropical understory environments, where there is keen competition for light and water. So they are quite at home in the extreme conditions of a house or apartment.

How much light you need to provide for your palms depends on the species. South- or east-facing windows are ideal. Light-loving species such as European fan palm, *Chamaerops humilis*, and Bismarck palm, *Bismarckia nobilis*, should be placed close to the windows. Those requiring less light, such as the many parlor palms, *Chamaedorea* species, and lady palms, *Rhapis* species, prefer broken or filtered light, but will tolerate indirect light. And the huge popularity of the kentia palm in the 19th century was due partially to its ability to grow in practically no light at all. If you live on the dim north side of your building and want to grow sun-loving palms, you will need to provide artificial light (see "Let There Be Light," page 91).

Most palms need abundant water but only a few tolerate soggy soil.

With their bold forms, palms add an architectural framework to the apartment conservatory. At right: *Dypsis lutescens*, butterfly palm.

PLANT SPECIFICS

Treat palms as you would other houseplants, watering them evenly and only when the soil is dry to a depth of one inch. If you are able to take your palms outdoors for the summer, you will need to water more frequently, depending on conditions.

Palms appreciate a good-quality potting mix. Look for a mix that provides good drainage. Palms do not mind being root-bound and can be kept in the same container for several years. When repotting, however, take care not to injure or cut the roots. What container to use depends greatly on your style of decorating, but it's often best to keep the palm in a plastic container and place this inside the decorative container of choice, as most do not allow for drainage.

Palms require only light fertilizing indoors. The best method is a timed-release fertilizer mixed with the potting soil, but you can use diluted liquid fertilizers at one-third the recommended rate during the growing season.

Remember that palms are basically unprunable and really just want to do one thing: grow up. It's difficult to shape a palm as you would boxwood, and pruning lower leaves will not make the plant grow faster. Trim off dead leaves only when they are brown and crispy.

PESTS

Now for the good news: most palms are practically pest-free in an indoor environment. The most crucial period comes when you bring your new palm home, because it may have pests that can infect your other plants. A good preventive treatment is to wash the leaves and stems with soapy water as soon as you bring the palm home. And you may want to treat a new palm as you would a new pet, keeping it away from the others for a while. After the quarantine period, you can move the palm into the general population.

THE BEST PALMS FOR INDOORS

DWARF SUGAR PALM *Arenga engleri*—A pinnate palm with dark green, glossy leaves. Stays small for some time. It can tolerate low light. Height: 8 feet.

BISMARCK PALM *Bismarckia nobilis*—Something of a challenge indoors because of its high light requirements, but the large silvery blue palmate leaves reward all the effort. Expensive, but worth it. Height: 6 feet.

PARLOR PALM *Chamaedorea elegans*—An heirloom palm as the common name implies, this clustering palm with pinnate leaves is one of the few that will bloom and fruit indoors, and its red berries add interest. Tolerates very low light. Height: 6 feet.

MINIATURE FISHTAIL PALM *Chamaedorea metallica*—This palm has entire (undivided) leaves. As the botanical name indicates, the leaves have a radiant silvery sheen. Excellent indoor palm; tolerates very low light. Height: 3 feet.

EUROPEAN FAN PALM *Chamaerops humilis*—The only palm native to Europe, this dwarf has silvery palmate leaves. Needs direct light. Height: 3 feet.

FISHTAIL PALM *Caryota mitis*—This palm is unusual for its bipinnate leaves, making it look like a huge carrot. Needs abundant light and space. Height: 10 feet.

BUTTERFLY PALM *Dypsis lutescens*—This pinnate palm is the one so frequently offered. Unfortunately, so many are crammed in one container that

Chamaedorea elegans, parlor palm.

Probably the most serious indoor pests are scale insects and spider mites. Scale insects are easy to control with a soapy cloth or, failing that, a light oil spray. Remember that scale insects will remain on the plant after they die, so you will have to rub them off for aesthetic reasons. Spider mites are best controlled through preventive maintenance, as they prey

they all suffer eventually. Try dividing so that there are only three or four per pot. You may or may not be successful. Needs good light. Height: 5 feet.

KENTIA PALM *Howea forsteriana*—The very best indoor palm, the kentia palm tolerates low light, dust, and low humidity. Deep green pinnate leaves make it resemble the coconut palm, which I do not recommend for indoors because of its high temperature and light requirements. Height: 6 feet.

RUFFLED FAN PALM *Licuala grandis*—The palmate leaves of this plant are held horizontally and form an almost perfect circle. Beautiful and unusual indoors. Needs medium light, moist conditions, and a warm location. This palm is very sensitive to fertilization and water, whether too much or too little. Height: 6 feet.

CHINESE FAN PALM *Livistona chinensis*—Another palm that is

Licuala grandis, ruffled fan palm.

usually crowded into its container with too many companions. It has shiny, deep green, palmate leaves. Tends to spread out before growing up. Needs good light and water. Height: 5 feet.

LADY PALMS *Rhapis excelsa, R. humilis*—These clustering palms with small, palmate leaves are very easy to grow indoors. They must have plenty of water or the leaf tips will burn. They will tolerate very low light conditions—in fact, they demand them. Height: 5 feet.

on under-fertilized, dry, stressed plants. To get rid of an existing infestation, use an oil spray. It's usually best to treat the palm again two or three weeks later to kill all larvae that have matured. (See also "Biological Pest Control in the Indoor Landscape," page 96.) If you take your palms outdoors during the warmer months, remember to allow them to harden off to the stronger light, and just as importantly, check for pests when you bring them back in. You may live in a high-rise building in the middle of a city, but spider mites will still know your address.

HOMESCAPING WITH PALMS

Probably the single most important contribution palms make to the apartment conservatory is architectural. A well-placed palm can make a small room seem larger and a large one more intimate. They also provide the anchoring structure for softer indoor plants such as crotons, dieffenbachias, and sanchezias. The large palm leaves also contrast well with smaller, finer-textured plants.

Palms are grouped into two basic categories based on their leaf structures. Palm leaves come in two basic shapes: fans (palmate) and feathers (pinnate). Each type provides its own kind of architecture. (See the box on pages 40–41 for the best palmate and pinnate specimens to grow indoors.)

Palms can complement any style of indoor gardening. Even if your taste doesn't run to the tropical and you prefer the more meditative effect of a Japanese garden or the classic lines of the Mediterranean, palms still are essential. It would be rare to find a temple garden in Japan without a windmill palm (*Trachycarpus fortunei*), and the French Riviera is thick with palms.

VARIETIES

Perhaps the most important factor in the indoor cultivation of palms is selection of the right variety. Many retail outlets choose palms not for their adaptability to an indoor environment but because they are inexpensive to grow and sell. These throwaway plants look good for a season or two but soon decline.

Knowledge is perhaps the best ally you can have. When you buy a palm for your indoor conservatory, you should know the species: since each species of palm differs slightly in its cultural requirements, you really can't take care of it until you know what it is. If the plant is not labeled properly (or at all), don't buy it.

With a minimum of effort, you can create a miniature tropical paradise that can allow you to escape from the pressures of the city and even feel as though you are in a garden rather than your living room. After all, that's the idea.

PLANT SPECIFICS

BAMBOO:

GRACEFUL GRASS OR JUNGLE GIANT?

SUSANNE LUCAS

IMAGINE YOURSELF ENCLOSED DEEP WITHIN A BAMBOO GROVE, a "living room" of green, with walls enveloping but breathing, a cathedral of vertical stems stretching to the heavens above, the shadows delicate and swaying. You feel quiet, contemplative and calm, protected. Are you in Kyoto, Bangkok, or Bali? No, you are at home, surrounded by bamboos in containers. It is not

There are a myriad of cultivated bamboo varieties with yellow, gold, burgundy, blue, and even black stems.

Many bamboos make wonderful indoor companions. There is a bamboo for almost any situation, from low light levels to bright sun.

difficult to create your own bamboo grove indoors—try it!

It could be said that bamboo is the most mysterious plant in the world. Once thought to belong among the most primitive of grasses, thanks to DNA analysis it has now been found to be one of the most highly evolved. Some species flower only once in a hundred years, while others bloom annually or sporadically. And, while bamboo has the reputation of being an invasive beast, an uncontrollable nuisance in the landscape, the cold-hardiest of the bamboos do not run at all, but rather form dense clumps from well-behaved root systems. What is more, bamboo isn't always a variation on the color green; there are a myriad of cultivated varieties with yellow, gold, burgundy, blue, and even black stems.

The term bamboo embraces a considerable diversity of plants, with representatives that grow only a few inches in height with vigorous rhizomatous root systems to giants of the tropics that can attain over 100 feet with woody, trunk-like stems rising from great clumps. Bamboos are forest grasses, and their life cycle, structure, ecology, and management must be understood within this context.

Many bamboos make wonderful indoor companions. There is a bamboo for almost any situation, from low light levels to bright sun. Because there are so many types to consider, and because their native homelands often have extreme climates, it is difficult to make rules that apply to all types of bamboo.

Bamboos that are grown for their height and culm character are more aesthetically pleasing and mimic greater age if the lower portion of the culm, or stem, is bare of branches.

CARING FOR BAMBOO

Bamboos are really no different from the more "usual" houseplants, and require the usual amenities: well-drained and nutrient-rich soil, sufficient light, adequate humidity, and fertilizer during the growing season. Because true bamboos are grasses, they love to eat. As flowering is rare and sometimes detrimental (consuming the plant's vigor), it is best to feed with a water-soluble high-nitrogen, low-phosphorus fertilizer, although really almost any balanced N-P-K fertilizer solution will do. Slow-release fertilizers like Osmocote 28-14-14 or Sierra 17-6-10 Plus Minors can be mixed into the soil for a complete feeding.

When growing bamboo in a container, be sure to use a pot with adequate room for this fast-growing plant. The container should be large enough to have a space at least two inches between the edge of the root ball and the side of the pot. Squatty tub-like containers are generally better than tall, deep ones, especially for the "running" bamboos with rhizomatous roots that typically grow more horizontally than deep. Any type of bamboo will spread within the container and eventually become potbound, but bamboos with clumping root systems do not outgrow their pots as quickly as running species. Once the bamboo completely fills the pot with roots and rhizomes, it needs to be moved to a larger container. Or, as with bonsai culture, its growth needs to be restricted: take the plant

continues on page 48

BAMBOOS FOR INDOORS

SMALL SPECIES

DWARF FERNLEAF BAMBOO, PYGMY BAMBOO *Pleioblastus pygmaeus* var. *distichus*—This low-growing bamboo species tops at 6 inches in height. Excellent container plant or groundcover within a mixed container planting.

TSUBOI BAMBOO *Pleioblastus variegatus* 'Tsuboi'—This temperate species is "grassy" in appearance, with small white-striped leaves. It has a running root system, is very vigorous, and grows up to 3 feet high. It does not tolerate hot sun, preferring lower light levels instead, though it will lose its vibrant variegation if it doesn't get enough light.

TINY FERN *Bambusa multiplex* 'Tiny Fern' or 'Golden Goddess'—A dwarf form of *B. multiplex* 'Riviereorum' with delicate, fern-like leaves. This temperate bamboo forms a clumping root ball and grows to 3 feet indoors. It is very adaptable to varying light conditions.

RICE-WRAPPER BAMBOO *Indocalamus tessellatus*—This temperate bamboo has very large, 15- to 20-inch long leaves, held downwards, and reaches a height of 3 feet. A very tough plant with a running root system, it tolerates very low light conditions and low humidity.

CHUSQUEA BAMBOO *Chusquea coronalis*—Elegant and delicate, *Chusquea coronalis* needs a cool, humid environment. Annual dormancy comes in September, as leaves turn orange and the plant partially defoliates. Grows to 4 feet with a clumping root system. Patience is required.

RADDIA BAMBOO *Raddia brasilensis*—A herbaceous bamboo of the tropical forest floor, *Raddia brasilensis* flowers continually. The leaves give it a fern-like appearance. The plant grows to 2 feet and needs indirect light. This running bamboo requires high humidity and supplemental chelated iron (to prevent chlorosis).

MEDIUM-HEIGHT SPECIES

MEXICAN WEEPING BAMBOO *Otatea acuminata*—The widely spaced culms of the lovely Mexican weeping bamboo get up to 1½ inches in diameter and grow to 12 feet tall. A tropical bamboo with a clumping root system. Tolerates full sun.

VARIEGATED TOOTSIK BAMBOO *Sinobambusa tootsik* f. *albostriata*—This temperate bamboo with variegated leaves grows very erect, with culms that are up to 1½ inches in diameter and up to 12 feet high. Prefers bright light and can be lightly pruned for a "topiary" effect. A running species.

SQUARE BAMBOO *Chimonobambusa quadrangularis*—Unique for its "square" stems, this temperate bamboo is very erect, with short branches and weeping leaves. It grows to 10 feet and needs moderate light levels.

SHIROSHIMA HIBANOBAMBUSA *Hibanobambusa tranquillans* 'Shiroshima'—For dramatic color, the variegated form 'Shiroshima' is fantastic, growing to 8 to10 feet with an architectural silhouette of branches stretching out half again as wide. Leaves are 6 inches long with many creamy white stripes. This temperate running species needs bright light.

TALL SPECIES

ALPHONSE KARR *Bambusa multiplex* 'Alphonse Karr'—Fountain-shaped 'Alphonse Karr' has 18-feet-tall, bright yellow stems up to 1½-inch thick, with green stripes. New shoots and stems are often reddish. Leaves are sometimes variegated white and green. It is heat- and sun-tolerant and forms a very tight root clump.

GIANT TIMBER BAMBOO *Bambusa oldhamii*—This tropical bamboo has erect green culms with relatively short branches. Stems grow up to 4 inches in diameter and 20 feet high. The large-leafed, clumping bamboo likes full sun and tolerates heat.

Hibanobambusa tranquillans 'Shiroshima'.

BUDDHA'S BELLY BAMBOO *Bambusa ventricosa*—If this species is kept dry and pot-bound, the internodes of its stems become swollen, which makes them look like Buddha's belly. It can grow to 20 feet; in its native habitat, this tropical clumping bamboo reaches a height of over 50 feet. It needs full sun.

BLACK BAMBOO *Phyllostachys nigra*—Black bamboo is a good candidate for containers because of its dark mahogany, almost black stems. As a temperate running species, it can drop many leaves each fall when days grow short. It may also suffer drying, burnt leaf tips due to low humidity, but this is offset by the beautiful stem color. Black bamboo can reach 20 feet indoors.

from the container, remove about a third of the roots, and replant it with fresh soil into the same container.

TROPICAL AND TEMPERATE TYPES

There are two types of bamboo, those that are native to tropical regions and those that grow in temperate zones. Temperate bamboo species are indigenous to climate zones that provide a period of cold dormancy. When grown indoors, a temperate bamboo may respond to the short daylight hours of winter by dropping some of its leaves and going semi-dormant. This is not damaging, but the plant can appear almost naked. During its "resting period," temperate bamboo prefers lower temperatures, ranging from 45 to 60° F., and requires very little water. This is important to note, as bamboos are very sensitive to overwatering.

Tropical bamboos are found in warm climates in which temperatures and daylight hours remain more or less consistent throughout the year. Tropical bamboos adjust to the indoor environment more easily. They, too, will react to gradual changes in daylight hours with sporadic leaf drop, but when temperatures and moisture are kept consistent, they will continue their growth cycles, especially with supplemental lighting.

PRUNING

The key to keeping bamboo beautiful is an occasional manicure. If you are growing a taller plant for its strong vertical culms, the proper name for the stems of woody grasses (it becomes a "cane" once it is cut), then regular thinning and pruning will keep it looking its best. Remove unwanted, "wimpy" or withered culms by cutting them off at soil level. Control the height of any culm by cutting just above the node (the place on the stem just above a branch). If the bamboo is stretching beyond what your ceiling allows, it will not suffer at all from being "topped." Simply cut the culm just above the topmost branch. Bamboos that are being grown for their height and culm character, benefit aesthetically and look older and more venerable if the lower portion of the culm is bare of branches. To emphasize the culm, remove branches that originate along the bottom-third, making sure not to leave "stubs," and shorten higher branches to the second node. Don't be afraid of pruning. Bamboo is tolerant and forgiving, and will appreciate the attention.

For that forest grove cathedral effect mentioned earlier, try large containers of *Bambusa ventricosa* or *Phyllostachys nigra*. If you'd prefer a more jungle-like effect, combine lower-growing forms with taller bamboos or with anthuriums, philodendrons, heliconias, passifloras, or whatever else strikes your fancy. Bamboos are compatible with many other types of plants. Container size and imagination are your only limits.

PLANT SPECIFICS

THE INDOOR ORANGERIE

TOM McCLENDON

IF YOU HAVE EVER WONDERED if you could grow citrus but live in a climate more suitable for apples, you are in very good company. Throughout history, people have endeavored to grow citrus indoors. The Romans grew lemons in greenhouses with mica windows. France's King Louis XIV was so smitten with the scent of orange blossoms that he had the first orangerie built and demanded that his gardeners have orange trees in bloom at all times. (They did, and I'll explain how later.)

In fact, the modern greenhouse owes its existence in large part to the orange. In the 18th century, as the British Empire grew, travelers who had acquired a taste of the subtropics began to build glasshouses just to grow citrus. The plants succeed well indoors if given good care. But it's important to know which varieties thrive in a relatively small indoor environment and why.

CAN'T I JUST PLANT A SEED?

Many people have wondered if they could grow a citrus tree from the seeds found inside tangerines, oranges, and grapefruit, and the

Dwarf citrus trees suited to growing indoors produce standard-size fruit.

49

Citrus are subtropical plants, and grow more or less all the time in their native regions. Most grow in flushes followed by several weeks in which the plants rest. Most indoor environments are warm enough to keep citrus growing nearly all the time, except during the coldest and darkest winter months.

simple answer is that you can. Citrus often come true to seed, and the seeds, if fresh, are easy to germinate. But you probably won't want to do this for a number of reasons. First, seedling citrus have a long juvenile period—often seven years or more—before they begin to flower and set fruit. Second, seedling trees often are very spiny. Citrus spines can be two or more inches long, which can present a hazard in your home. Finally, seedling trees are often spindly and leggy and grow taller than is practical in an indoor environment.

Most citrus grown for home use are dwarf varieties that are either cutting-grown or grafted on a dwarfing rootstock such as the trifoliate orange *(Poncirus trifoliata),* a citrus relative. By using cuttings or grafts from mature trees, the grower produces a plant that is ready to begin fruiting right away. Grafting on dwarfing rootstock keeps the plant small, but the good news is that the fruit is not dwarfed. A dwarf 'Navel' orange produces fruit every bit as large and tasty as a standard tree, though not in the same quantity.

When choosing a variety, try to pick one that performs well indoors and for which the grower can provide reliable information. You should know if the variety has been grafted, because if the scion (top) dies, the undesirable rootstock will take over and the tree will be useless. If the grower does not know whether the plant has been grafted, look at the trunk of the tree about six inches above the surface of the soil. If there is a swollen area above which the trunk bends away toward the soil at a slight angle, the plant has been grafted.

ORANGES OR LEMONS?

Citrus can be broken down into two basic categories, sweet and acid. Sweet citrus such as oranges and tangerines need abundant heat to ripen fully, which is why they are difficult to grow in cooler climate areas that would seem perfect for citrus, such as San Francisco. So much heat is required for grapefruit to ripen, for example, that in cooler parts of California the fruit must stay on the tree for more than 18 months.

Sweet citrus will therefore be difficult to grow successfully at home. However, it can be done, especially if you are able to take the tree outside for the summer months. You will also need to be very patient.

Much easier to grow indoors are the acid citrus such as lemons and limes. Some citrus such as the Calamondin do so well indoors that they seem to prefer this environment. Acid citrus will ripen fruit much faster and will tend to be nearly ever-blooming.

Don't be surprised if your citrus sheds a lot of immature fruit after blooming. Like many fruits, citrus produce many more fruits than the plants can support. So there is nothing much to worry about if your plant drops surplus fruit, provided it is otherwise healthy.

HIGH CULTURE

While commercial citrus are grown in full sun for maximum fruiting, it is surprising how little light citrus will tolerate outdoors. Outside, they need only about four hours of sun for good growth and fruiting. Indoors, however, citrus will need more abundant light than many homes can provide, particularly during the growing season.

During the winter citrus can tolerate low levels of light as long as they are kept fairly dry. They will go dormant if kept dry and at temperatures around 55° F., though fruit will still ripen. In fact, Louis XIV's gardeners used an extreme form of this method to keep the monarch happy. By starving citrus to the point of defoliation and then applying water, they would trick the orange trees into bursting into bloom year-round.

Citrus are subtropical plants, and grow more or less all the time in subtropical regions. Most grow in flushes followed by periods of several weeks in which the plants rest. Most indoor environments are warm enough to keep citrus growing nearly all the time, except during the

PLANT SPECIFICS

coldest and darkest winter months. With many varieties—especially acid citrus—it is not unusual for the plant to bear three or four crops a year.

During the growing season citrus appreciate water and humidity, though they are surprisingly tolerant of neglect—to a point. Fortunately, drought stress shows up fairly quickly on these plants and is easily remedied. However, citrus cannot stand overwatering, and if the soil is continuously wet the plants will succumb to root rot. Water citrus as you would other houseplants, letting the soil get a little dry on top before watering again. The best thing to do is to keep the humidity level high around the plant by regularly misting the leaves.

Citrus respond quickly to fertilizer, and any nutrient deficiencies show up quickly. Fortunately, applying a liquid 20-20-20 fertilizer at half-strength during the growing season will keep your citrus plant happy.

UNUSUAL CITRUS VARIETIES THAT THRIVE INDOORS

CALAMONDIN *Fortunella japonica*—The plants have wide, lush leaves and bright orange fruit that resemble small tangerines, though they remain sour.

KAFFIR LIME *Citrus hystrix*—A lime-type tree, Kaffir lime has the added bonus of having delicious leaves used in cooking Southeast Asian dishes.

LIMEQUAT *Citrus aurantiifolia* × *Fortunella crassifolia*—This plant is a cross between a Key lime and a kumquat. The fruit is about the size of an egg and a beautiful clear yellow. These plants also are relatively cold-hardy, able to stand temperatures in the mid-20s F. without damage.

MANDARIN ORANGE *Citrus reticulata* 'Blanco'—This "orange" isn't really an orange at all but a mandarin. Like other mandarins it requires far less heat to ripen than true oranges, and the fruit

Fortunella japonica, Calamondin.

PESTS

The good news for indoor citrus enthusiasts is that there are few pests that attack citrus indoors, and that combatting those that do is directly related to the health of the plant. Spider mites are one of the worst pests. They love plants that are dry and under-fertilized, so you can keep them away by keeping your citrus well watered and well fed. Scales are another citrus pest.

There are more troubling pests, but their occurrence in indoor citrus is rare. The Asian leaf miner is a small creature that burrows into the undersides of leaves, making them twisted and deformed. Oil spray will kill miners but you will also want to remove and (preferably) burn infected leaves. Aphids can occasionally infest citrus. They cluster near new growth and suck plant juices—particularly from emerging leaves and stems. Again, an oil spray or wash will usually control these pests. (See also "Biological Pest Control in the Indoor Landscape," page 96.)

PLANT SPECIFICS

on a Mandarin orange is deliciously sweet.

MEIWA KUMQUAT *Fortunella crassifolia*—Much different from the oblong and tart kumquats commonly found at the market, Meiwa kumquats are round and sweet, perfect for fresh eating.

MEYER LEMON *Citrus meyeri*—This lemon is perfectly suited for container culture and will bear heavily with a minimum of effort on your part. The lemons are deep yellow with a good flavor, though a little sweet.

OROBLANCO GRAPEFRUIT *Citrus paradisi* × *C. maxima*—Though not particularly sweet, grapefruit does require lots of heat to ripen.

Citrus meyeri, Meyer lemon.

Oroblanco is a cross between a grapefruit and a pomelo, which doesn't require as much heat to become sweet.

CACTI AND OTHER SUCCULENTS

JULIA SOLARZ

IT'S WINTER. SNOW FALLS. Your breath rises frosty in the air. Bundled up beyond recognition, you find yourself longing for warmer regions. Arizona's Sonoran Desert would do nicely. Perhaps a trek through Namaqualand, South Africa. Not in the cards? Then, why not bring the desert to you? Create a little heat and drama right in your own living room with potted cacti and succulents.

Succulents evoke glorious warmth, while ranging widely (and wildly) in form and texture from the bold, columnar magnificence of *Cereus* and euphorbias to the exquisite, flower-like forms of aeoniums, aloes and echeverias and the rounded shapes of mammillaria and rebutia cacti. *Nolina recurvata* (ponytail palm), a slow-growing member of the Agave family, evokes images of otherworldly landscapes, with its strange, swollen base and palm-like leaves. The slender leaves of *Dasylirion longissimum* arch to form a graceful fountain. Some succulents, like *Sedum morganianum*, cascade in voluptuous rivulets from hanging or wall-mounted pots.

Viewed alone, succulents become minimalist sculpture. Grouped together, they mirror vast desert scenery. Leaf and stem colors range from the white and deep-green zebra stripes of *Haworthia attenuata* to the lavender-tinted leaves of striking, orange-blossomed *Echeveria peacockii*. Many cacti also produce startling flowers in saturated hues. An echinopsis cactus crowned with a show-stopping blaze of huge apricot or red-orange blooms is breathtaking.

Opposite: Cacti and succulents work in any setting from casual to formal. Paired with art objects, they are as intriguing as sculpture.

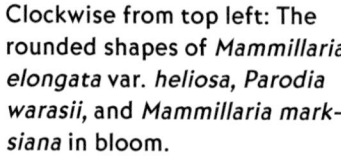

Clockwise from top left: The rounded shapes of *Mammillaria elongata* var. *heliosa, Parodia warasii,* and *Mammillaria marksiana* in bloom.
Bottom: *Haworthia attenuata.*

EXPLAINING SUCCULENTS

Succulents form a large group of plants with modified structures that enable them to store water and withstand drought. Special cells in their leaves, stems, or roots collect and hold water, releasing it into the plant when needed. Horticulturists use the term "succulents" to describe any of the many plants with these exceptional water-retaining properties. Many different kinds of plants—cacti, euphorbias, and agaves among them—are gathered under the umbrella term of succulents.

POTTING

The way succulents are potted can be the difference between success and failure. First, the pot you choose must be clean, have a good drainage hole, and should be in proportion to the size of the plant. Clay pots are ideal because they are porous, allowing the soil to dry out more quickly and the succulent's roots to get needed air circulation. Pots made from glazed ceramics, galvanized steel, and other materials will also work. Just remember that the soil in these pots will dry out more slowly, so you will need to water them less frequently.

Next, choose the right planting medium. A good, fast-draining, nursery-bought cactus mix works well; regular potting mix doesn't drain fast enough. You can also make your own soil mix by blending equal parts of

Top: When repotting a spiny succulent, it's best to wear gloves
and use tongs.
Bottom: a collection of small
succulents.

indoor potting mix with pu-
mice, perlite, vermiculite, or
coarse sand.

The tools you need for
repotting a spiny succulent are
heavy gloves, a pair of tongs,
and a rolled-up newspaper or
bath towel to hold the plant in
place while you are pouring
soil into the pot. First, place
one square inch or so of plastic
screening (the type that's used
to cover windows) over the
drainage hole of your pot.
Don't use broken pottery or
rocks; they can clog the
drainage hole. Next, scatter a
handful of pea gravel over the
bottom of the pot for extra
drainage. Add soil mix one
third of the way up the pot,
pressing the soil lightly with
your fingers without compact-

ing it. Then, slightly tilt the plastic nursery pot housing your cactus or succulent and gently squeeze it, loosening the plant, root ball, and soil from the
pot. Using the tools if you're handling a prickly cactus or heavy gloves for
other succulents, lift the plant from the nursery pot. Brush a small amount
of rooting hormone on the root tips. Carefully position the plant in the new
pot and add soil up to the base of the plant, making sure not to bury any
green. The succulent's base should be about an inch below the rim of the
pot.

Gently compress the soil with trowel or fingers. Cover with a thin layer
of pea gravel to weight down the light cactus mix. Use a light brush to

PLANT
SPECIFICS

Many plants familiar to the gardener—including cacti, euphorbias, and agaves—are technically succulents.

remove any bits of soil from the plant itself. Avoid transplanting a succulent when it is in flower, or it may lose its bloom.

LIGHT REQUIREMENTS

To grow succulents successfully indoors, it is essential to match the light requirements of the plants with the available light in the space where you choose to display them. Though most succulents need ample light, it is a mistake to assume they all can tolerate strong, direct sunlight. Some, especially cacti (with the exception of the epiphytic species), do require a full blast of sun for at least four hours a day, preferably from a south-facing window, but many other succulents thrive best on strong indirect light. If you're placing succulents in front of a window with southern, western, or eastern exposure, it's a good idea to use blinds to slightly diffuse the light, or display your plants a little further back in the room, away from the window. All plants grow toward the light. Succulents are no exception, so turn them once in a while to prevent a lopsided growth pattern, but be careful of sunburn to the previously shaded side.

If you've got little or no sunlight, don't despair. Handsome sansevierias are the perfect choice for you. The snake plant, *Sansevieria trifasciata*, has stiff and erect sword-like leaves up to four feet long and three inches wide. The leaves are dark green with light green striping. Two other choices for lower light levels include *Euphorbia trigona* and *Euphorbia lactea*. Succulents can also be grown under Gro-lux fluorescent or HID grow lights placed about two feet above the plants.

Succulents have modified stem and leaf structures that enable them to store water and withstand drought.

WATER, FOOD, AND TEMPERATURE

The key to watering cacti and and other succulents is restraint. Err on the side of too little rather than too much. Understanding how they behave in the wild may help you in this regard. Succulents have adapted to an environment with little water. Most receive rainfall only in a concentrated period of time during spring, when they put out slow, new growth and also flower. The rainy season is followed by a long, dry period in which the plants are dormant. With this in mind, water and drain your plants well during the period of active growth (usually spring and summer), allowing the soil to thoroughly dry out before watering again. Once a week is usually adequate. Succulents are adapted to handle some neglect, so an occasional two weeks without water won't hurt them. Taper off watering to once a month during fall and winter when most succulents are dormant. It is best not to water your succulent at least a week before and after transplanting.

One effective way to test soil moisture is the "cake test method." Slide a narrow wooden skewer into the soil near the rim of your pot. Push the skewer to the bottom of the pot, then pull it out. If the skewer is dry, it's time to water. If the skewer is at all moist or if wet soil clings to the skewer, the plant doesn't need water.

Always water thoroughly near the rim of the pot, keeping the water away from direct contact with the plant. Rather than using a dish to catch excess water, try watering them in the sink or bathtub, allowing the soil to drain thoroughly before replacing the plant in its usual location. If the succulent is too large to move, a dish may become a necessity. If so, water the soil a little at a time. Wait a minute or so, then repeat until a small amount drains into the dish. Absorb this excess with a paper towel.

Indoors, succulents grow more slowly than outdoors, and they do not respond well to overfeeding. Unless the needs of a specific plant suggest otherwise, use an all-purpose liquid fertilizer diluted to one-quarter strength once a month during the growing season (usually March through August) and not at all in other months.

Ideally, temperatures should mirror those in the deserts where most succulents grow wild: warm days (in winter your heater will do if it is not too close to the plants) and about a ten-degree drop in temperature at night for healthy growth and bud formation. However, succulents are forgiving and will tolerate some deviation from this pattern. Desert plants also need fresh, circulating air. Leave windows partly open at least part of the day during milder weather.

ARRANGEMENTS

Cacti and succulents work in any setting from casual to formal, Southwestern to East Indian. If you'd like an arrangement of cacti with a sense of humor and whimsy, try combining separately potted, hairy or spiny cacti in separate pots. Pair Mexican old-man cactus, *Cephalocereus senilis*, or peanut cactus, *Echinopsis chamaecereus,* and *Cleistocactus strausii* with bizarrely shaped cacti like *Opuntia microdasys* 'Crest' and the brain cactus *Mammillaria elongata* 'Crest'.

Some indoor gardeners like collecting small, rare cacti for a windowsill display. These are a little more difficult to care for. Some examples of this type are any of the ariocarpus, small, rock-colored cacti with wart-like markings; turbinicarpus, tiny barrel cacti with soft, bent spines and white or pink flowers; and *Astrophytum asterias*, with its low, rounded, spineless body divided into eight flat ribs with small white flecks.

Dish gardens are also captivating; a mix of small plants in one shallow container can recreate a desert scene on a small scale. The best choices for these containers are slow-growing succulents. It is wise not to combine cacti and succulents because of their different light requirements. A layer of shells or tumbled glass pebbles makes an attractive soil covering. Some people like to mix art objects with succulents. And, placed alone, bold *Euphorbia grandicornis* or *Cereus* with their exaggerated forms are as intriguing as any sculpture (though, because they grow so tall, you may be forced to prune them after a while). As far as design goes, the only rule is to choose succulents that perform well indoors and are grouped in a location that meets their light requirements.

PLANT SPECIFICS

GODS AND MONSTERS:
THE GENUS FICUS

SCOTT D. APPELL

WE ENCOUNTER GLORIOUS SPECIMENS in ubiquitous bank and shopping mall plantings, we marvel at lush archetypes on tropical isles whilst on vacation, and we regard forlorn examples in the corners of our doctor's office. We adore them. We despise them—yet we attempt to maintain them time and time again. They are the gods and monsters of the indoor gardening world— they are the figs, the rubber trees, the genus *Ficus.*

Since the 1880s, these plants have formed the most important group of trees and shrubs that can be successfully cultivated indoors. They add height and volume to an otherwise low landscape, and their various leaf textures and colors and bark characteristics perk up a monotonous "leafy" collection. They can be trained as indoor espaliers and topiaries, pruned into space-dividing hedges or screens, coaxed along living room arbors and trellises, or

Ficus benjamina 'Variegata', a form of the immensely popular weeping fig.

The genus name *Ficus* is the Latin name for the edible fig.

gently trimmed to retain a pleasing natural appearance. In addition, the small-leafed vining species can be grown as groundcovers with larger potted plants, in Wardian cases and terrariums, or around obelisks, finials, or wattle shapes.

The genus name *Ficus* is the Latin name for the edible fig. Most *Ficus* species are evergreen, but some are completely deciduous (such as *Ficus carica*), depending on seasonal temperatures and rainfall. Many species have large and extraordinarily beautiful foliage, which varies in color, texture, venation, and margination. Others have remarkably small, delicate leaves. Almost all species produce a thick, milky latex when cut or wounded. In fact, the viscous sap of several species has been utilized in the manufacture of rubber, hence the common name, "rubber tree."

GROWING FIGS

All *Ficus* species are very sensitive to over- or underwatering, which causes yellowing of the foliage and often complete leaf-drop. Even the remaining green leaves may plummet. The key to growing figs successfully is to allow them to dry out almost completely (especially in apartments with chilly hibernal temperatures) before saturating them. Never let the pots sit in excess run-off water. Large containers may even need to sit on pot feet within their drainage saucer in order to achieve this ideal. Drafts and low temperatures may induce similar symptoms. The temperature and light requirements of *Ficus* vary according to species, depending on the conditions in its native habitat.

RESUSCITATING FICUS

Many the lament I have heard from the rubber tree owner who has returned home from a *brief* vacation to find his or her tree completely leafless, the victim of a benevolent neighbor or other plant-sitter. One or two poorly timed waterings had sent the poor plant into deciduous shock! As long as the leafless stems and branches of a *Ficus* in shock remain supple, they are capable of sprouting new foliage. If the soil is dry, give the plant a thorough watering. Never fertilize your leafless charge(s) with the assumption that a dose of plant food will help them "come 'round." This will only send them over the edge. Sadly, figs with kindling-dry twigs and snapping branches are candidates for the compost pile, wood chipper, or Department of Sanitation. *—SDA*

Feel free to repot *Ficus* when they become pot-bound—every two to three years. (*Ficus elastica*, however, doesn't mind a snug fit.) Figs prefer a light, fast-draining soil of medium fertility, and do well in both compost-based or soilless mixtures. Truly large specimens that cannot be potted up into a larger container must rely on annual bouts of top-dressing—the process by which several inches of the top-most soil is removed and subsequently replaced with a fresh, fertile nutrient-enhanced mixture. Top-dress annually in late February, when the plants begin their spring growth cycle. Regular applications of your favorite water-soluble fertilizer are beneficial as well.

In addition, figs benefit from a thorough feather-dusting or wiping-off with a damp, lint-free cloth or sponge. If the plants are not too large or unwieldy, a lukewarm shower in the bath-tub is effective. Try maintaining your plants on dollies or caddies for easy maneuvering. Never use any type of leaf polishing agent, including olive oil.

Ficus are susceptible to all of the standard indoor arthropod pests: mealy bugs, spider mites, and both soft and hard scale insects. Employ your favorite biological controls (see "Biological Pest Control in the Indoor Landscape," page 96).

For the past quarter century, the figs have been workhorses in the interior landscape industry. Surprisingly, many interior landscapers, novice and amateur alike, believe there is nothing new in the world of *Ficus*. They couldn't be more wrong! New selections have flooded the market and are readily available; the selections that follow are ample proof.

FICUS FOR INDOORS

BENJAMIN FIG, WEEPING FIG
Ficus benjamina—Weeping fig is one of the most popular house-plants in the U.S. It has a graceful, open, slightly weeping form as well as thinly leathery, symmetric, ovate-elliptic (oval to egg-shaped) 3- to 5-inch leaves. It grows as tall as 12 to 15 feet, and can be maintained with 250 foot-candles of light, but prefers 4,000 to 6,000. *F. benjamina* is extremely drought-tolerant. There is a vast assortment of varieties and cultivars from which to select, including ruffled and variegated forms. 'Midnight Princess' is a notable cultivar, which bears long, dark leaves that have undulating crenate (with rounded teeth) leaf margins.

Ficus elastica 'Burgundy'.

INDIA RUBBER TREE *Ficus elastica*—By far the most prosaic *Ficus* species is *Ficus elastica*, the ubiquitous India rubber tree. It can be expected to reach ceiling-height in any indoor landscape. The leaves are a foot or so long, elliptic to oblong in shape, thick, dark green and leathery, but glossy on the upper surface. *Ficus elastica*, which is surprisingly drought-tolerant, can be sustained with as little as 250 foot-candles, although 4,000 to 8,000 will result in far better growth. There is an array of cultivars; 'Melany' produces deep green, truly miniature leaves with brilliant burgundy overtones.

FIDDLE-LEAF FIG *Ficus lyrata*—Another large-leaved *Ficus* is the fiddle-leaf fig. Its foliage, as large as 18 inches long and a foot wide, and obovate to lyrate (lyre-shaped) or pandurate (fiddle-shaped), makes this plant easily recognizable. The leaf texture is rough and leathery. With proper care, this species can easily reach ceiling-height. Selective pruning will help attain a pleasing shape. It can be maintained under 250 foot-candles, but prefers 2,000 to 6,000 for optimum growth. It is not particularly drought-tolerant, and must be given water regularly to survive; but do not let the pot stand in the excess run-off water. The extremely rare but striking variegated cultivar 'Ivonne' bears leaves with a green and gray-green center surrounded by a variable ivory margin.

BANANA-LEAF FIG *Ficus maclellandi*—During the 1980s, *F. maclellandi* was introduced by two leaders of the indoor landscape industry, Kraft Gardens, Inc., and Aloha Foliage. The former gave it the common name banana-leaf fig, while the latter received a trademark for the name 'Alii'. The word, correctly written *Ali'i*, is Hawaiian for "royalty." This plant has a heavier trunk, sheds fewer leaves, and appears to be far more durable than *F. benjamina*. It has long, narrow, slightly weeping, willow-like foliage, and can quickly attain a height of 14 feet indoors. It is exceptionally drought-tolerant. 'Alii' tolerates light as low as 200 foot-candles, but it prefers 4,000 to 6,000. No cultivars.

INDIAN LAUREL *Ficus microcarpa (F. retusa, F. nitida)*—A little more difficult to find commercially is the Indian laurel. It bears handsome 3- to 5-inch dark green leaves that are long and broadly elliptic (oval). The bark can be a light gray to almost white in color. This species can tolerate exceptionally cool indoor winter temperatures without any yellowing or leaf-drop. It recovers from hard pruning quite well, making it a good candidate for indoor hedges, screens, or espaliers. It

can be maintained under 300 foot-candles but prefers 4,000 to 6,000. There are several cultivars.

MISTLETOE FIG *Ficus deltoidea (F. diversifolia)*—An easy-to-care-for shrub for the indoor landscape is the mistletoe fig. The outstanding foliage, though variable, usually has an interesting fan-like shape. The leaves are held on slender zigzagging branches. This is one of the few *Ficus* species to develop fruit indoors, and the inedible, yellow or ivory fruit is very persistent. This species can eventually achieve a height of 3 to 5 feet. It cherishes heat and humidity and is quite intolerant of draughts and overwatering. It can be sustained under 250 foot-candles but prefers at least 4,000. Currently, there are no cultivars.

CLOWN FIG, MOSAIC FIG *Ficus aspera* 'Parcellii'—One of the most spectacular *Ficus* species available today is the variegated form of *Ficus aspera*, the cultivar 'Parcellii'. It is usually a large shrub or small tree, and may attain a height of 3 to 5 feet in ideal conditions. The foliage is 8 to 12 inches in length, cordate (heart-shaped at base) to rhomboid (like a lozenge) in shape, and sometimes coarsely toothed on the margins. The leaves are a sensational combination of white speckling or marbleizing and

FICUS FOR INDOORS, CONTINUED

Ficus aspera 'Parcellii', clown fig.

gray-green blotches on a dark green background. Some leaves may be pure white. In perfect conditions, the plant bears pink to purple figs. This *Ficus* requires heat and humidity, and detests cold and drafts. It needs at least 3,000 foot-candles to prosper. Use room temperature (warm) water only, and tip out the run-off, especially in a cool room.

CREEPING FIG *Ficus pumila (F. repens)*—The best known of the vining species of *Ficus*, this beloved houseplant is a great choice for poorly insulated homes and apartments. It is a fast and vigorous grower, bearing 1- to 2-inch soft green leaves. It can be easily trained upon sphagnum moss-filled topiary shapes, osmunda fiber poles, or wooden frames, and it is a perfect groundcover for larger containers, Wardian cases, and terrariums. Creeping fig also makes a handsome choice for

hanging pots or raised planters. It suffers greatly when overwatered, but can be successfully cultivated under 350 foot-candles. Several cultivars are readily available, including 'Minima', whose especially tiny foliage makes it an attractive subject for tracery against light-colored walls.

OAK-LEAFED FIG *Ficus montana (F. quercifolia)*—Another small-leafed climbing *Ficus*, very similar to the creeping fig, except its tiny 1- to 1 ½-inch leaves have irregularly dented margins, making them look decidedly like oak leaves. It's a little slower growing than the creeping fig, but a perfect diminutive plant to incorporate in eye-level planters, terrariums, or moss or osmunda fiber topiary forms. It prefers at least 350 foot-candles of light. Avoid overwatering. The choice cultivar 'Snowflake' has a variable variegation of pure white.

FICUS SAGITTATA (no common name)—For a coarser-textured vining fig, try *Ficus sagittata*, The foliage is 2 to 3 inches in length and held on wiry, trailing stems. Like the aforementioned climbing species, *F. sagittata* resents overwatering. The cultivar 'Variegata' is quite wonderful, though difficult to find. It has gray-green leaves variegated with creamy white and makes an effective groundcover or topiary.

PLANT SPECIFICS

AT HOME WITH FERNS

MOBEE WEINSTEIN

IF YOU FIND YOURSELF FASCINATED WITH FERNS, congratulate yourself. You are among a select group of people described as follows by Herbert Stansfield in the mid 1800s: "The bright colors in flowers are admired by the least intellectual, but the beauty of form and textures requires a higher degree of mental perception and more intellect for its proper appreciation."

Growing ferns indoors first became popular in England in the 1800s, and reached its peak in the 1850s, during the so-called Victorian Fern Craze. Fern cultivation was a highly fashionable fad, which arose purely for aesthetic reasons. Fortunately, technological developments in heating and the manufacture of glass coincided, allowing people to pursue their new passion. The intense preoccupation with ferns further stimulated academic studies, and scientific interest was also fostered by improvements in microscopes and their greater availability. As in other sciences, in fashion,

Nephrolepis exaltata,
Boston fern.

A fern dish garden planted with *Pteris multifida*, *Asplenium nidus*, and *Pellaea rotundifolia* (from left to right).

music, dance, and the other arts, horticultural trends cycle around, coming in and going out of style. Presently these "semi-antique" plants are enjoying a revival, much like heirloom vegetable and flower varieties.

To most people, the word "fern" conjures up certain images—delicate, lacy, airy greenery luxuriating in a shady little spot. While this may be true for some ferns, these plants are more diverse than most people think. Ferns originated about 300 million years ago, and there are about 12,000 species of ferns and fern allies growing on the earth today. Their leaves vary in size from ⅛ inch to 60 feet, and their colors range through the full spectrum of green and also white, silver, golden yellow, red, pink, copper, and burgundy, even blue. Fern fronds come in different textures and can be thick and leathery, somewhat succulent, hairy, waxy, or super thin—only a single cell layer thick! The majority of ferns make their homes in moist tropical forests, but they also venture into cold temperate zones, bodies of water, and even the desert. These somewhat primitive plants do not flower or set seed, but rather reproduce by spores. However, they do have a vascular system, a relatively advanced feature, which is basically a network of veins for the transport of water, nutrients, and food. Their stems are often modified into "rhizomes"; at times these are very obvious and showy, and at other times they're hidden in the soil.

From a design perspective, ferns are very versatile. Their quiet, graceful beauty lends itself equally well to classical, formal styles and rustic, informal settings. A perfect example is the Boston fern, the most common fern grown in America today.

GROWING FERNS

Most people shy away from growing ferns, thinking that they are all too difficult. However, with proper selection and care, they are very gratifying plants.

Victorian growth chambers were needed to provide humidity, but also to maintain warmth and protect plants from the noxious fumes of coal heating.

INDOOR FERNERY

HUMIDITY

With many ferns, humidity is the key to success. Most require at least 35 percent; 40 to 50 percent is even better. The typical home has 10 to 25 percent, especially in winter, and in summer as well if an air conditioning system is being used.

Humidity is a relative factor, hence the term "relative humidity" (RH). Cooler air has less of a capacity for holding moisture than warmer air. With the same amount of actual moisture in the air, 55° F. will have a higher relative humidity reading than 65° F. So you begin to see why keeping plants cooler, especially in winter, is beneficial. There are several things you can do to increase the humidity around your plants. Running a humidifier will produce the best results, and it's also good for you, your wood furniture, books, paintings, and so on. Mass or group your plants together, and/or set them on trays of gravel filled with water, but be certain to raise the bottom of your containers above the water level. Add a few pieces of charcoal to the tray, and clean it thoroughly with a 10-percent bleach solution or scalding water every two months or so.

You can also mist ferns with larger leaves, but bear in mind that one little spritzing a day won't increase humidity for very long—when the droplets have dried up, the humidity is basically gone! An alternative is to enclose your plants in a terrarium of some kind. Fancy growth chambers date back to Victorian England. At the time they were needed not only to provide humidity, but also to maintain warmth and protect plants from the fumes of the burning coal that was used as a heating fuel. Now such growth chambers are sometimes used to provide additional warmth, but mainly to maintain humidity.

TEMPERATURE

The majority of ferns that are available to us as houseplants originate
continues on page 72

PLANT SPECIFICS

FERNS FOR INDOORS

ROUGH MAIDENHAIR *Adiantum hispidulum*—A terrestrial clump-forming fern 8 to 12 inches tall, this species is not as delicate as the common maidenhair, but has an interesting frond shape. Young leaves emerge copper-colored and mature to green.

MOTHER FERN *Asplenium bulbiferum*—This terrestrial, clump-forming fern has medium green, somewhat fleshy, dissected leaves. One of the "mother ferns," it produces baby plantlets on its leaves, making it easy to propagate.

BIRD'S NEST FERN *Asplenium nidus*—Naturally an epiphyte, this fern can grow up to 3 feet (usually 1 foot). The leathery, strap-shaped fronds are bright green and form a nice rosette.

Davallia fejeensis, rabbit's foot fern.

ROCHFORD HOLLY FERN *Cyrtomium falcatum* 'Rochfordianum'—This terrestrial clump former grows to about 1 foot. Decorative, glossy, dark green leaves have toothed edges resembling holly.

RABBIT'S FOOT FERN *Davallia* species—These epiphytic ferns have fronds 1 to 2 feet long and fuzzy rhizomes. Their leaves are usually very finely dissected. Excellent for hanging baskets.

SQUIRREL'S OR BEAR'S FOOT FERN *Humata tyermannii*—This epiphyte strongly resembles *Davallia*, but it is smaller, with fronds 8 to 12 inches, and has more slender, whitish colored rhizomes. It might be a little easier to grow.

JAPANESE CLIMBING FERN *Lygodium japonicum*—A terrestrial clump-forming fern with twining stems climbing 5 feet (to 20 feet). Wiry stalks support hand-shaped segments. Cut down old growth to avoid a large, tangled mass.

SWORD FERN *Nephrolepis cordifolia*—This clump former can be grown terrestrially or epiphytically, but with erect fronds it is best as a potted plant. This species is more sturdy and tolerant of low light than the common Boston fern type, *Nephrolepis exaltata*.

BUTTON FERN *Pellaea rotundifolia*—This terrestrial fern forms clumps with leaves 8 inches long. It is a charming potted plant with very dark green, somewhat glossy, small, rounded leaflets resembling buttons.

HARE'S FOOT FERN *Phlebodium* species—An epiphyte, this plant can be grown potted or in a hanging basket. Fronds are variable from 1 to 4 feet long and bright green to steel blue-gray. The stout creeping rhizomes are covered with orange-colored scales.

STAGHORN FERN *Platycerium* species—This epiphyte is best grown in a basket or mounted on cork or wood slabs. These bizarre, curious plants resemble stag's antlers and are very interesting and decorative.

TSUS-SIMA HOLLY FERN *Polystichum tsus-simense*—A terrestrial clump former 8 to 12 inches high. Its very attractive stiff, leathery, somewhat glossy dark green leaves have black veins and bristly tips.

WHISK FERN *Psilotum nudum*—Naturally terrestrial and epiphytic, this plant, which is not a true fern, grows in a clump 6 to 18 inches high. A curiosity, this primitive plant has no true roots or leaves; it consists of a bunch of green, forking stems.

BRAKE FERN *Pteris* species—Terrestrial clump formers, members of this genus are very variable in size (8 to 24 inches) and leaf shape, which is usually nicely dissected. Some are variegated with white or silver. The fertile (spore-bearing) fronds are distinct in shape. The very common Cretan brake prefers lime in the soil as do some others.

LEATHER LEAF *Rumohra adiantiformis*—A terrestrial clump-forming species that grows 1 to 1½ feet. It has very shiny dark green, leathery leaves.

TREE FERN *Cyathea (Sphaeropteris)* and other tree ferns— Tree ferns are palm-like in habit. They are elegant but delicate and must not dry out.

Pellaea rotundifolia, button fern.

in the tropics and prefer a daytime temperature ranging from 65 to 75° F.; the nighttime temperature should be 10 degrees cooler, ranging from 55 to 65° F.

LIGHT

Contrary to what many people think, ferns do not grow in the dark! They are photosynthetic creatures just like other plants. Ideally, ferns prefer bright, indirect light for best growth, and many will benefit from a little sun in winter. Many will tolerate lower light, but under these conditions, they merely survive and won't grow very much.

SOIL MIXES

When it comes to potting and soil mixes, it is useful to divide ferns into two categories: terrestrial and epiphytic. Terrestrial ferns grow naturally in the ground and make good potted plants. For these ferns, use a soft, organic soil mix such as: 2 parts loam, 2 parts organic matter (leaf mold, compost, or peat moss), 1 part perlite, 1 part vermiculite, 1 part charcoal, and 1 part very fine grade orchid bark. Ferns tend to have small, delicate root systems, so when potting, don't disturb the root ball too much and firm the soil in place, but don't "pack" it in.

Epiphytes naturally grow up in trees, or on rocks, etc., not in the earth. Most epiphytic ferns have an extensive rhizome system that grows around their "support structure." The rhizomes will grow all around your basket or pot, so they should be "planted" on the surface and then allowed to grow "outside" the container. Epiphytes require a different mix: 1 part of the terrestrial mix above combined with ½ part of very fine grade orchid bark and ½ part tree fern fiber.

PESTS

The most common pests on ferns are scale and mealybug. Picking mealybug off by hand or with a Q-tip dipped in alcohol or soapy water is very effective, although tedious. Scale is even more difficult to remove manually. Another non-chemical control is to release some beneficial, predatory insects. (See "Biological Pest Control in the Indoor Landscape," page 96).

PROPAGATION

Propagating many ferns is easy. Those that grow in a clump can be divided using typical methods. Many epiphytes can be propagated from rhizome (stem) cuttings. These take best if the pieces have at least one leaf and preferably roots. Some ferns, commonly called "mother ferns," make baby plantlets along their leaves, and these can easily be separated and grown in a separate pot. Most ferns can also be grown from spores, which is not as difficult as it may sound, but takes much longer.

PLANT SPECIFICS

MORE INDOOR LANDSCAPE PLANTS

SCOTT D. APPELL

TREES AND SHRUBS

ARALIAS

Members of the genus *Polyscias* include the plants commonly called aralias. Most make splendid, though *not* carefree indoor plants. The foliage is often tripinnate (compound leaf branching twice) and very attractive. These plants require good air circulation, humidity, and twice-monthly feedings during active growth. They demand even moisture but resent overwatering. Aralias are slow-growing and lend themselves particularly well to specialized pruning techniques, attaining an indoor height of 5 to 7 feet. *Polyscias* species and cultivars are surprisingly tolerant of low light, and can be grown successfully with as little as 125 foot-candles, but variegated cultivars will excel with 1,500.

Schefflera arboricola 'Variegata'.

SCHEFFLERA

The popular *Schefflera actinophylla*, the schefflera or umbrella tree, has been grown for many years as a houseplant, while *Schefflera arboricola* (dwarf schefflera) has been of major importance since

Araucaria heterophylla.

NORFOLK ISLAND PINE

Araucaria heterophylla, Norfolk Island pine, is one of the few gymnosperms to adapt to interior cultivation. It has a pine tree-like appearance, and is often sold in December as an "indoor Christmas tree." It tolerates 300 to 5,000 foot-candles, and temperatures ranging from 45 to 90° F. Another species, *A. bidwillii,* the Bunya-Bunya pine, produces more coarse-textured, spiny, broad-needled foliage. Both species may reach 6 feet under ideal conditions indoors. They will not tolerate top pruning of the terminal growth. Araucarias need fresh circulating air and plenty of moisture. Periodic room-temperature showers to remove dust and soot prove beneficial as well. Compost-rich soil is another essential.

CORDYLINES AND DRACAENAS

Cultivated indoors since the 1860s, the ubiquitous dracaenas are forgiving in nature, lush in appearance, fast growing, and affordable. They range in size from tabletop varieties to plants 20 feet tall. Dracaenas tolerate temperatures as low as 40° F. These plants perform better when underwatered than when overwatered, and are sensitive to chlorine and fluoride poisoning.

Cordyline terminalis, the red-edge dracaena, is one of the most popular indoor foliage plants. This species grows slowly to ceiling height with slender, flexible, picturesquely contorted, light-colored trunks. The foliage is linear and

the mid 1970s. They both produce palmately compound (like the fingers of a hand), glossy dark green foliage, the former with leaves 1 to 2½ feet wide, the latter with leaves 2 to 7 inches wide. Both species prefer full sun for optimum growth—5,000 to 7,000 foot-candles is ideal, but they will survive with as little as 600. They require a well-aerated and fertile potting mix kept moist but not soggy. They are surprisingly resilient to temperature fluctuations, and will withstand 35 to 105° F. without chilling or heat damage, although 65 to 90° F. is optimal. A humidity level of 60 to 80 percent is welcomed as well. The umbrella tree can easily attain ceiling-height, and the dwarf schefflera, a slower grower, may reach 7 to 8 feet in height.

narrow—about 18 inches long and less than an inch wide, and will be stiffly erect with full sun, or droopily arched with insufficient light. The plants grow with as little as 150 foot-candles, but excel with 2,000 foot-candles.

The well-known corn plant, *D. fragrans,* has somewhat leathery, dark green leaves about 3 feet long and 3 to 4 inches wide. It will flower in cultivation, producing long pendulous panicles of vanilla-scented tubular blooms. Another "corn plant," *D. deremensis*, bears dark green leaves, 2 to 3 feet long by 2 to 3 inches wide.

YUCCAS

The spineless yucca, *Yucca elephantipes,* often reaches 30 or 40 feet in the wild, although it rarely reaches ceiling height indoors. The deep green foliage is 2 to 3 feet long, and as much as 4 inches wide at the base. The leaves are spiny-pointed, but relatively soft-tipped. This architectural plant is a perfect addition to the cactus and succulent garden. Although they can be maintained with as little as 150 foot-candles, they will flourish with 5,000. They are very drought-tolerant, but resent overwatering. Yuccas can withstand temperature fluctuations from the upper 30s to 90° F.

PODOCARPUS

The big-leaf podocarpus, *Podocarpus macrophyllus,* is a conifer with dark green, flat leaves that are loosely arranged in spirals. They bear a slight resemblance to their distant

Top: *Dracaena deremensis* 'Lemon lime'.
Bottom: *D. fragrans.*

Spathiphyllum wallisii.

hildmannianus can be maintained with as little as 200 foot-candles, they will flourish with 6,000. A rich, but flawlessly drained soil is required. Allow them to dry out completely between waterings, and never let them sit in a saucer of excess run-off water. The flowers are white, 6 inches in diameter, and extremely fragrant.

HERBACEOUS PLANTS AND VINES

SPATHIPHYLLUM
Often called the "peace lily," this aroid is arguably the most important indoor landscape plant available. The leaves are oblong-lanceolate (oval to lance-shaped) and dark green, and the flowers are pure white and single-stalked. The natural flowering season is February through June. The peace lily will perform in all but the darkest locations—75 foot-candles is the minimum, but 150 is better. Although it will produce copious foliage, spathiphyllum will not bloom with too many foot-candles. It prefers temperatures between 65 and 85° F., and should be kept slightly moist.

cousins, the yews. They are incorporated into sundry dish gardens or terrariums, but 6- or 7-foot specimens are readily available. Podocarpus are easily maintained with as little as 500 foot-candles. They prefer a moist but well-drained, loam-based potting mix and plenty of fresh air. Winter temperatures should be on the cool side, not over 72° F. Frequent misting or showering of the leaves is beneficial.

PERUVIAN APPLE CACTUS
This true cactus is easily recognized by its columnar shape and 5 to 8 plump ribs bearing areoles, from which the spines arise. It is a perfect addition to the cactus and succulent garden. Although *Cereus*

ASPIDISTRA
Once regarded as the symbol of full middle-class respectability, the aspidistra was a workhorse of the Victorian parlor garden. This hardy foliage plant supports long, glossy green, lanceolate (lance-shaped) leaves on stiffly upright stalks. It makes a perfect large groundcover or specimen plant. Aspidistras will survive with as lit-

tle as 25 foot-candles, but prefer 75 to 100. They tolerate wide fluctuations in temperatures as well, 23 to 100° F., and are extremely resistant to dust and pollution. Their main drawback is their frustratingly slow rate of growth. Maintain them in a fertile, well-drained medium that is kept on the dry side during the period of winter dormancy.

PHILODENDRONS

These herbaceous tropical aroids prefer a rich, humusy but well-drained soil. They definitely have visible growing seasons: they are in active growth during the summer months, when they enjoy warm temperatures—65 to 85° F. During this time, water and fertilize your philodendrons liberally. The plants slow down during fall and winter, when temperatures should be cooler, and you should withhold fertilizer completely. Don't overwater during this period. Although philodendrons may be maintained with as little as 150 foot-candles, some of the new hybrids demand 1,500 to 2,500 foot-candles. Most philodendrons are distinctly vine-like.

Philodendron bipinnatifidum.

GRAPE IVY

The grape ivy, *Cissus rhombifolia,* is a common houseplant indeed, but few people use it to its best advantage. With its shiny green, dentate (with teeth along the margin), trifoliate (having three leaflets) leaves, it is one of the best vines for indoors. Grape ivy uses its grape-like tendrils to climb upwards, and may be employed to cover indoor arbors and trellises, which is how it was used by Victorian gardeners, or utilized as living room dividers or wall covers. It requires about 1,200 foot-candles for best performance, but will tolerate as little as 75. It prefers temperatures between 68 and 82° F. Grape ivy likes somewhat acidic soil with a pH level of 5.5 to 6.2. Provide a rich but well-drained soil mixture containing peat moss, and keep it slightly moist.

GROWING TIPS

FROM THE GROUND UP:
SOIL MIXES AND FERTILIZERS

MOBEE WEINSTEIN

GROWING PLANTS IN CONTAINERS is an ancient practice, which is perhaps at its peak of popularity today. For most indoor gardeners, plants are confined to pots of some kind. This unnatural setting presents us with special considerations warranting a closer look at the growing medium and how it supports plant life.

Naturally, soil is a dynamic thing in a state of constant change. It consists of mineral, or inorganic particles, organic matter, water, air, and a variety of living organisms. In order for a growing medium to support good plant growth, it must provide four things: water, air, nutrients, and physical support. Water retention is intimately associated with aeration. The growing medium must hold water and be porous in order to make air available. Often, water retention and aeration are mistaken as contradictory conditions. It is not only possible but essential to achieve both simultaneously. Plants also require certain nutrients in order to grow and thrive. Carbon, oxygen, and hydrogen are primarily supplied by air and water; the other essential elements, however, are generally absorbed from the growing medium. Lastly, the medium provides a place for the roots to anchor, offering physical support for the plant.

There are two basic categories of growing media: soil-based and soilless. Soilless mixes are also referred to as "synthetic" soils, but don't interpret this to mean that they are artificial. Typically, all of the ingredients are completely natural. Obviously, there is some soil in a soil-based mix, but none in a soilless one. As long as the four basic requirements of a medium are met, it almost doesn't matter what goes into it. When decid-

For most indoor gardeners, plants are confined to containers—an unnatural setting warranting a closer look at the growing medium and how it supports plant life.

ing which type you want to use, one major consideration is weight. Soil-based media are generally much heavier than soilless ones. If you have a large, top-heavy plant, such as a small tree, then you may need the weight to keep the pot from toppling over.

Another thing to consider is that when you start with a sealed bag of a soilless mix, it will be free of contaminants like diseases, insects, weed seeds, and so on. There are so many materials available for mixes that it makes sense to take a closer look at them. For the most part, materials will either be used for their water and nutrient retention properties or for their aeration quality. There are a few exceptions: coarse grade bark, calcined clay, and vermiculite provide both.

MATERIALS WITH GOOD WATER AND NUTRIENT RETENTION

SOIL

Soil, preferably loam (a type of soil characterized by approximately equal amounts of sand, silt, and clay), has very good retention properties. It should be pasteurized for most indoor uses. (See box on page 82.)

ORGANIC MATTER

SPHAGNUM PEAT MOSS: Sphagnum peat moss has a very high water-holding capacity and good nutrient retention. It's a stable form of organic matter, decomposing slowly, which means that it will last a long time, and not tie up soil nitrogen. (The microorganisms that break down organic matter require nitrogen, hence rapid or very active decomposition requires a lot of nitrogen. This depletes the soil's nitrogen supply and can starve plants.) It's very acidic, usually with a pH range of three to four. Leave it "chunky"; better structure yields better aeration and it will take longer to break down.

BARK: Many types of bark are available. Redwood and fir bark are found on the West Coast, pine is common on the East Coast and in the Gulf states, and hardwood is typical of the interior states. Bark is often cheaper than other types of organic matter. Before using bark in a growing mix, you must compost it. This will bring it to a stage where further decomposition will be steady but slow and nitrogen tie-up will not be a problem. It will also enhance the nutrient-holding capacity and destroy naturally occurring compounds which can be injurious to plants. This process can take anywhere from four months to one year.

MANURE: Rotted cow manure is the best, but it should be pasteurized to eliminate diseases, weed seeds, and so on. As an added bonus, it provides some nutrients, especially micronutrients.

COMPOST: Compost can be made up of many different materials. It's an excellent soil conditioner and a good way to recycle kitchen and yard waste and it usually provides some nutrients. Leaf mold is a particular type of compost, made up of decomposing leaves; it is very common in areas with cold winters and a lot of deciduous trees.

SAWDUST: Sawdust is in some ways similar to bark. It must also be partially composted for the same reasons. However, sawdust doesn't last long, as it decomposes very quickly, tying up nitrogen in the process. For these reasons I wouldn't recommend using it.

STRAW: Straw needs to be chopped into small pieces before being added to a soil mix. For the reasons mentioned under sawdust, I do not recommend using straw in a soil mix either.

MATERIALS PROVIDING GOOD AERATION

SAND

Sharp, coarse-textured sand is excellent for drainage and aeration, but it is heavy and provides no other function. Try to get washed sand; it's more uniform in size, and cleaner. Never use beach sand or sand that's used on roads in areas with cold winters. These sands will most likely contain salts that can burn your plants.

PERLITE

Perlite is volcanic rock whose particles are "popped" under extreme heat. It's more expensive than sand, but very lightweight. Water is held on its surface, and it is basically sterile, and nearly neutral in pH.

POLYSTYRENE FOAM

This is the only synthetic material in the list. Styrofoam is probably the best known brand. Polystyrene foam is a good substitute for sand. Very much like perlite, it is extremely lightweight but often cheaper. Usually, it is derived from scraps that are leftover from the manufacture of other products. As technology and recycling efforts continue and improve, other useful synthetic materials created as by-products or salvaged from waste materials may become available in the future.

MATERIALS PROVIDING GOOD WATER AND NUTRIENT RETENTION, AERATION, AND DRAINAGE

CALCINED CLAY

Aggregates of clay particles are heated to high temperatures to form hardened particles that resist breaking down. Not only does this material provide good drainage and aeration, but it also has good water and nutrient retention. Unfortunately, it is expensive.

VERMICULITE

Vermiculite is a type of mica whose particles are "exploded" into an accordion-like structure under high temperatures and pressure. In addition to providing good drainage and aeration, it has a high capacity for water and nutrient retention. It also provides a few essential elements and is very lightweight. The downside is that it's typically more expensive than perlite and that it's easily compressed, which means you will lose aeration over time. It should generally not be used with soil, as the weight of the soil will be enough to compress it.

RECIPE: SOILLESS MIX FOR FOLIAGE PLANTS

FOR ONE BUSHEL OF MIX: Combine ½ part peat moss with ¼ vermiculite and ¼ perlite. To this add 3½ ounces of 5-10-10 fertilizer, ¾ ounce of iron sulfate, and 5¾ ounces of ground limestone.

FOR ONE GALLON OF MIX: Combine ½ part peat moss with ¼ vermiculite and ¼ perlite, as above. To this add ½ ounce of 5-10-10 fertilizer, a pinch of iron sulfate, and ¾ ounce of ground limestone.

THE RIGHT MIX

A typical soil-based mix is made up of equal parts loam, coarse sand, and peat moss or another form of organic matter. This medium is perfectly suitable, but keep in mind that it will most likely be "contaminated," as explained above, and that it will be heavy. You should pasteurize it before use. (See box below.) More and more growers today rely on soilless media. These were originally created to overcome the wide variability in soils and problems with insects, diseases, and weed seeds. In the 1950s, the University of California pioneered the development of these mixes in America. Named "UC mixes," they ranged from 100 percent sphagnum peat moss to 100 percent fine sand with a range of combinations in between. The most popular is the half peat moss, half fine sand mixture. In the early 1960s, Cornell University introduced two "Peat-Lite mixes." One is a mixture of half peat moss, half horticultural grade vermiculite; the other contains perlite instead of the vermiculite. Many soilless mixes also contain added nutrients, lime, and sometimes wetting agents.

Today, there are many brands of ready-made mixes to choose from. You may already be familiar with some of them: Jiffy Mix, Pro-Mix, Redi-Earth, Metro Mix, Sunshine Mix, to name a few. As the UC and Peat-Lite mixes, most are very simple formulations, and it is easy to mix your own if you wish. (See recipes on pages 81, 85). Most large garden centers carry both premade mixes and the individual ingredients. For most home gardeners, it is certainly easier and sometimes cheaper to purchase a product that is ready to go. (When doing so, look for an open bag so that you can inspect a sample first.) If you need a large quantity and have plenty of space for mixing and storing, it may be worthwhile to make your own. It will probably be cheaper.

RECIPE: PASTEURIZING SOIL

Spread a 4-inch layer of moist soil in a metal baking pan and cover tightly with aluminum foil. Insert a meat thermometer through the foil and into the soil. Set the oven on a low setting (275° F.) and slide the pan into the oven. Once the thermometer reaches 160 to180° F., let the soil cure for ½ hour. Don't let the soil temperature exceed 180° F. or you will destroy beneficial organisms as well.

1 gallon of soil will take about 30 to 40 minutes at 275° F., ½ bushel will take about 1½ hours. Let the soil cool for 24 hours before using.

NOTE: Some people find the smell somewhat unpleasant, so don't do it just before company is coming!

TEXTURE, STRUCTURE, AND DRAINAGE

Whatever you decide, remember that drainage and aeration should be your main concerns. The texture of a soil is determined by the relative amounts of the three mineral particles: sand, silt, and clay (listed in order of decreasing grain size). As everyone knows, sand drains very quickly but it doesn't hold moisture and nutrients. While this may solve the problem of poor drainage and aeration, it poses a new problem: a reduced capacity for water retention. This is why the soil structure—the way individual particles bond together to form aggregates, or clumps—is an important consideration. With the help of organic matter, the structure of the soil can be adjusted so that it provides good aeration as well as good water retention.

It is interesting to note that soil drainage is directly proportional to the depth of the soil that lies above the water table. In a container, the bottom is equivalent to the water table. Therefore, a pot that's eight inches high will drain better and more quickly than a pot that's two inches high, which will present a rather swampy condition just after watering, as it is similar to field soil two inches above freestanding water (the water table).

It's also important to note that when you are preparing a medium for longer term use, you should add no more than 10 percent organic matter. Initially, a mix with a higher organic content might be excellent, but as time passes and the organic matter decays, the soil will compact, losing its porosity. To avoid the problem, raise the amounts of sand or better, perlite or calcined clay. Don't use vermiculite, as it compresses too easily. Obviously, the medium will provide fewer nutrients and will require more judicious fertilizing.

FERTILIZERS AND OTHER ADDITIVES

WETTING AGENTS

Anyone who's ever worked with peat moss knows that it is very difficult to wet when it is dry. Some of the commercially prepared mixes contain wetting agents, which help the peat moss to absorb water. Unfortunately, these are often difficult for the home gardener to obtain.

PH LEVEL

pH is a measure of acidity or alkalinity, with seven indicating neutral. Most of our garden plants prefer to grow within the range of 6.2 to 6.8; acid-loving plants prefer 5.0 to 5.8. A soil test will determine the pH of your medium and if necessary, adjustments can be made. You can raise the pH by adding ground, dolomitic limestone at the rate of five to ten pounds per cubic yard of a soilless medium and a little under five to ten pounds for every cubic yard of a soil-based one. (This translates to 16 to

GROWING TIPS

20 ounces for every three bushels or a good, heaping teaspoon per six-inch pot.) To lower the pH, you can add aluminum sulfate, or even better, iron sulfate. To use iron sulfate, drench the soil in your containers thoroughly with one tablespoon of iron sulfate per gallon of water.

CHARCOAL

Charcoal is very absorbent and is well known to most people as a filtering agent. Like sand, perlite and vermiculite, it comes in different grades (particle sizes). Larger, coarser grades will help to open up the medium, but the main purpose of charcoal is to help purify the medium, keeping it "healthy" by absorbing any possible toxins and reducing pH fluctuations.

FERTILIZERS

Soilless mixes generally have little or no nutrients available to plants, therefore they require the addition of a general-purpose fertilizer. Such a fertilizer will contain sufficient amounts of all three macronutrients: nitrogen (N), phosphorus (P), and potassium (K), represented by the three numbers on a fertilizer label. One simple recommendation is to add five pounds of 5-10-10 fertilizer per cubic yard of mix. (In most cases, fertilizer should not be added to the mix if it is going to be stored for a while.)You might also want to add a trace element mix at the rate of two ounces per cubic yard. This will supply a full complement of micronutrients. Soil-based media rarely require a trace element supplement.

Another option is to fertilize on a regular basis, every two weeks, usually beginning in mid-February and ending in mid-September for most indoor plants, using a liquid fertilizer (water-soluble) at half-strength. Or you can use a controlled-release fertilizer. I choose a for-

QUICK CONVERSIONS FOR RECOMMENDED RATES

- 5 lbs. per cubic yard = 3¾ ounces per bushel = ½ ounce per gallon
- 5 to10 lbs. per cubic yard = 3¾ to 7½ ounces per bushel = ½ to 1 ounce per gallon
- 2 ounces per cubic yard = ½ teaspoon per bushel = a pinch per gallon

NOTE:
- 1 cubic yard = 22 bushels
- 1 bushel = 8 gallons
- 1 bushel is approximately 1¼ cubic feet, or a box that measures 13 inches by 13 inches by 13 inches.

mula that will last the whole growing season and therefore only need to apply it once in the spring. Organic fertilizers originate from living organisms, as opposed to synthetic ones, which are derived from inorganic chemicals. Despite their different origins, plants will ultimately absorb these nutrients in the same form. Common organic fertilizers include bone meal, cottonseed meal, blood meal, fish emulsion, and sewage sludge. Typically, they act more slowly than synthetic ones and last longer, which means that it's more difficult to over-fertilize or burn. However, you usually need greater quantities, which means more bulk and weight and often more expense. Manure is sometimes used as a fertilizer, but it contains rather low amounts of nutrients and is much more useful as a soil conditioner.

RECIPE: SOILLESS MIX FOR TREES AND SHRUBS

FOR ONE BUSHEL OF MIX:
Combine $\frac{2}{3}$ part ground bark and $\frac{1}{3}$ part fine sand. To this add $3\frac{3}{4}$ ounces of 5-10-10 fertilizer, $\frac{3}{4}$ ounce of iron sulfate and $5\frac{1}{4}$ ounces of ground limestone.

FOR ONE GALLON OF MIX:
Combine $\frac{2}{3}$ part ground bark and $\frac{1}{3}$ part fine sand, as above. To this add $\frac{1}{2}$ ounce of 5-10-10 fertilizer, a pinch of iron sulfate and a scant $\frac{3}{4}$ ounce of ground limestone.

POLYMERS

Water-absorbing polymers are relatively new compounds that deserve mentioning. These synthetic "crystals" become gel-like and are able to absorb up to several hundred times their volume in water. They can be added to soil mixes to greatly improve water retention. Since they have a great capacity to swell, mix them into your soil, then moisten before filling your containers.

Now that you're armed with a fundamental knowledge of soils, dig in and get your hands dirty. Remember to start at the bottom, because much of your plant's health and well-being depends on the medium that it's growing in.

GROWING TIPS

PLANTS DON'T WANT LITTLE SIPS OF WATER HERE AND THERE. They like a long, satisfying drink. If you water a plant incompletely, you encourage root growth only in the portion of soil that has been watered. This usually means roots grow in the soil at the top of the container, where the soil receives moisture, instead of more deeply and throughout the pot. Water until excess water runs out the drainage holes of the plant's container.

In fact, every plant requires this kind of complete watering, from the moisture-loving anthurium to the desert cactus, from the small specimen in the two-inch pot to the three-foot planter box. What varies is the optimum frequency of watering, which is determined by several variables: the type of plant; the temperature, light, and humidity levels of its environment; its stage of growth; and the size and material of its container.

Plants give visual clues to their watering needs: succulents have fleshy leaves with thick cuticles. Fleshy leaves indicate the ability to store water in leaf tissue—consider the burro's tail (*Sedum morganianum,* page 87, top) or the partridge-breast aloe (*Aloe variegata*). Other plants, while not technically succulents, may also have thick leaves and cuticles, and are therefore relatively drought-tolerant, like most members of the genus hoya, many peperomias, and even phalaenopsis orchids. Cacti have modified foliage (spines) and specialized storage tissue that allow them to go without water for long periods of time. Conversely, plants that have delicate, thin leaves with little or no cuticle lose more water more quickly through transpiration, making specimens like the peace lily (*Spathiphyllum* species, page 87, bottom) and the peacock plant (*Calathea makoyana*) higher maintenance houseplants.

If you place smaller plants around the bases of trees and/or have large

masses of various species, be sure to group plants with similar watering needs together. Don't underplant a large pencil cactus (*Euphorbia tirucalli*) with thirsty rex begonia vine (*Cissus discolor*). You certainly may combine desert and rainforest plants in the same landscape, but give them separate containers.

CREATING A PLANT-FRIENDLY ENVIRONMENT

Top: Fleshy leaves indicate the ability to store water in leaf tissues.
Bottom: Thin delicate leaves with little or no cuticle lose water more quickly.

You've probably noticed that your plants require less frequent watering in winter. This is a function of reduced temperatures and shorter daylight hours. In early spring, most tropical plants (that's to say virtually all our houseplants) begin to grow more rapidly, in response to longer hours of daylight and warmer temperatures. As they enter this stage of active growth, they require more water, more light, and more carbon dioxide.

Similarly, plants in north-facing windows require water less frequently than those in south-facing windows because the lower light and temperature levels of northern exposures result in slower growth.

When arranging different plants together in one container, be sure to choose species with similar watering needs. A desert dweller like *Euphorbia tirucalli*, pencil cactus, makes a bad pot mate for a rainforest plant.

Many city apartments are too warm and dry for humans and plants alike, which translates into more frequent waterings for your houseplants. If you can control your own thermostat, consider maintaining a nighttime temperature of 60 to 65°F. and a daytime temperature of 70°F. Your houseplants will require water less frequently and will be less stressed by heat and dryness.

Arranging plants in groups is an excellent way to increase ambient humidity. The air in a fully landscaped interior can have much higher humidity than a room with few or no plants. As one plant loses water to transpiration, that moisture passes into the surrounding air. Other nearby plants benefit from the moist air and contribute to it as they, in turn, transpire. When numerous plants are grouped in a single area the air becomes more humid; each plant loses less water to the surrounding air and requires less frequent watering. Increased humidity is healthier and more comfortable for the human inhabitants of your landscape as well.

You might also consider raising ambient humidity by incorporating "dry wells" into your interior landscape. A dry well is a tray or saucer of pebbles placed underneath the pot of a plant. Keep the pebbles covered with water, just up to the level of the bottom of the pot. As the water evaporates from underneath and around the pebbles, it humidifies the air around the plants and reduces their need for water.

Gardening under artificial light increases your plants' need for water. The lights generate heat, which dries out container soil, and longer light hours speed up photosynthesis and transpiration. The closer the lights are to the plant material, the more frequently you will need to water.

The size and type of the pots you choose for your interior landscape will also affect the amount of water your plants will require. The smaller the container, the smaller the volume of soil and water it can hold. Therefore, a small pot needs watering more frequently than a larger container, since

If you'd like to combine a thirsty rain-forest plant like *Cissus discolor*, rex begonia vine, with plants that have different water requirements, remember to give them separate pots.

it cannot hold as much water between its soil particles. Additionally, a pot made from a porous material such as clay or wood will lose water via evaporation through the container walls, as well as through the soil surface. Containers made from non-porous materials such as plastic or metal will lose water through the soil surface, but will need less frequent watering since water does not evaporate through the container walls. Glazed clay falls somewhere in the middle, with the porosity of the clay being tempered by the non-porosity of the glaze.

TOOLS FOR WATERING

There are several alternatives to the traditional watering can, and you can choose your tool according to your personal style. An indoor hose with a wand attachment can be hooked up to your sink with an inexpensive adapter. Hoses are light-weight and come in many lengths. Wands may be used for watering or misting. For hanging plants you might consider using a plastic squeeze bottle and curved tube combination, allowing you to water without taking baskets down. The traditional watering can itself remains a handy tool. Any can should have a smooth flow of water; a long narrow spout will allow you to place the water exactly where you want it, without spilling or wetting foliage.

Permanent plantings, such as walls of ferns or orchids, may be misted frequently instead of watered in the traditional manner. Consider placing a humidifier close to the epiphytes. And for a thorough foliage soaking, use a two to three gallon pump sprayer containing water or a mixture of water and fertilizer.

Keep in mind that several chemicals in tap water are harmful to certain plants. Many communities in the U.S. add fluoride to their water (approximately 0.5 to 1 ppm). Unfortunately, some of our most common house-

Before watering plants sensitive to chlorine, like *Kalanchoe,* it's best to let tap water sit for 24 hours or use a filter.

plants are very easily damaged by fluoride, including *Chlorophytum* species, *Cordyline terminalis,* and *Dracaena deremensis* (especially 'Souvenir de Schriever' and 'Janet Craig'). *Maranta* species, *Spathiphyllum* species, and *Ctenanthe* species are equally sensitive. A potting mix with a high pH level may reduce your plants' uptake of fluoride, but if your water is heavily fluoridated, you may need to reconsider growing many plants in the Lily and Maranta families.

Chlorine is not usually present in concentrations high enough to damage plants, but certain species such as *Kalanchoe* and *Tradescantia* are particularly sensitive. Use a water filter to remove chlorine from tap water (but not fluoride), or let your tap water sit for 24 hours to allow the chlorine to escape. This provides the added benefit of warming your tap water to room temperature. Cold water shocks roots, and over time this can stunt growth and weaken the general health of your plants, making them susceptible to disease. Also, cold water on leaves can cause foliage spots. Remember, while human beings may not relish a drink of tepid water, your plants most certainly prefer it.

The key to successful watering is the ability to correctly gauge how frequently you must water, not how much water you should give your plant. Each plant will have its own optimum watering schedule, which you will establish by careful observation of the above criteria. A general rule of thumb is that houseplants in containers less than 12 inches in diameter need water when the top inch of soil feels dry to the touch. Stick your finger into the soil, and if it feels dry down to the first knuckle, it's time to water. Large trees and plants in containers more than 14 inches in diameter should be judged by a different standard: the top two to three inches of soil can feel dry to the touch before these plants require watering.

Over time and with care you will learn how frequently your plants need water, but at the start you might consider using an inexpensive water meter. A slim metal probe attached to a meter measures soil moisture. Be sure to take readings from several different spots in the soil. While a water meter may help you learn about the individual needs of each plant, there is no substitute for careful observation. Consistent care and attention on your part will always be essential to the health of your plants.

LET THERE BE LIGHT

ELLEN ZACHOS

MY FIRST APARTMENT IN MANHATTAN was a third-floor studio with one barred window that looked across a narrow shaft to a brick wall. In other words, the apartment was dark. Did this keep me from growing orchids, starting ferns from spores, or propagating tropical vines? Not for a New York minute!

There have been enormous innovations and improvements in artificial light in the past five to ten years, so the absence of natural light should not limit your interior landscape. There are three characteristics of light to consider when you're deciding which type of bulb to use: color, intensity, and duration.

COLOR: While the sun emits light in all colors of the visible spectrum, light in the blue and red ranges is most important for plant growth. Flowering plants need large amounts of orange/red light in order to bloom, and blue light promotes lush, compact growth of foliage plants.

This timer-controlled light fixture runs with metal halide or high-pressure sodium bulbs.

CALCULATING FOOT-CANDLES

With a single lens reflex (SLR) camera, set the film speed to ASA 25 and the shutter speed to ⅟₆₀th of a second. Focus on a white sheet of paper or cardboard in the area where you want to measure the light intensity. For each F-stop setting there is a corresponding approximation of foot-candles, listed below:

F-STOP	FOOT-CANDLES
2	100
2.8	200
4	370
5.6	750
8	1,500
11	2,800
16	5,000

INTENSITY: Light intensity is measured in foot-candles, which is defined as the strength of light given off by one candle at a distance of one foot. Light intensity is the single most important factor in photosynthesis. Less than optimum light intensity may not kill a plant, but will result in leggy, weak growth, or inhibit flowering and fruiting. Consider that outdoors on a sunny day light intensity measures approximately 10,000 foot-candles. Even a sunny room has much less intense light, about 3,500 foot-candles. (See box at left for an easy way to measure light intensity using a camera.)

DURATION: This refers to the number of hours of light per day. If your landscape includes primarily foliage plants with some blooming species, 14 to 16 hours a day is plenty. Other plants require longer exposure in order to flower and set fruit. Since artificial light doesn't exactly duplicate the intensity of sunlight, you need to compensate by giving plants more hours of artificial light than they would receive in their native habitats. Remember that most plants need a period of rest/darkness. Photosynthesis occurs in the presence of light and results in the creation of glucose, i.e. food, but it is the respiration process, which continues after dark, that lets plants break down the glucose into usable forms.

LAMPS, LIGHT MOVERS, AND REFLECTORS

Once you've determined what kind of light you need, you can choose among several different types of fixtures. The brightest lamps available are high intensity discharge (HID) lights, which can be installed anywhere in your home, garage or greenhouse to supplement existing light or as the sole source of light for your plants. These bulbs pass electricity through a glass or ceramic tube containing a mixture of gases; the blend of gases determines the color of the light given off by each type of lamp.

High intensity discharge lamps can be divided into two subcategories:

metal halide and high-pressure sodium. Both types emit a considerably more intense light than the more familiar fluorescent lamp, which also passes electricity through a gas-filled tube.

All HID lights can run on regular 110V household current but require special fixtures with ballasts. A horizontally oriented ballast will run 25 percent cooler and therefore last longer than a vertically oriented ballast. Make sure all electrical equipment meets Underwriters Laboratories (U/L) standards; it should be recommended as safe for use in damp conditions and around water.

Metal halide (MH) bulbs give off light that is strongest at the blue end of the spectrum and looks most like natural sunlight. It produces compact, leafy growth and is preferable when your indoor garden is an integral part of your home, since the light does not distort the colors of the plants (and people) it illuminates. Metal halide bulbs need to be replaced about once a year and are less expensive than high-pressure sodium bulbs.

High-pressure sodium (HPS) bulbs last about twice as long as metal halide lamps but cost slightly more. HPS lamps emit a light strong at the red/orange end of the spectrum and promote flowering and fruiting; but bear in mind that their light has a red/orange cast and distorts the colors of everything it illuminates. They may also produce leggy growth unless used in conjunction with natural light or a metal halide system.

You can use both HPS and MH lamps in a single location, but a metal halide bulb cannot be used in a high-pressure sodium fixture, and vice versa. If you are using multiple fixtures, consider a combination of HPS and MH systems. If you have only one fixture, you may use a

CALCULATING WATTAGE

When determining how much wattage you need, first calculate how much space you want to illuminate. A light mover increases the square footage you can light with a single lamp; as a rule, you'll want 20 to 40 watts per square foot of garden. Divide the wattage of your bulb by 20 (e.g. $1000 \div 20 = 50$), then divide the wattage of your bulb by 40 (e.g. $1000 \div 40 = 25$). This will give you the extremes of your light intensity range. With one 1000-watt system, you can light between 25 and 50 square feet of interior landscape, depending on the plants' light requirements. You can adjust your setup as you observe how well your plants grow, moving plants or the light fixture to increase or decrease the light intensity to meet the individual plants' needs. Do not, however, change the bulb in your lamp to a bulb with more watts. Each fixture is designed for a specific wattage, and a 400-watt bulb cannot operate safely in a 250-watt system.

GROWING TIPS

conversion bulb. A metal halide fixture can be fitted with a conversion bulb that emits a sodium-type light; conversion bulbs are available in all sizes for halide fixtures. There is only one size of conversion bulb for the reverse conversion: a 400-watt halide conversion bulb operates in a 400-watt HPS system.

INDOOR PLANT LIGHTING

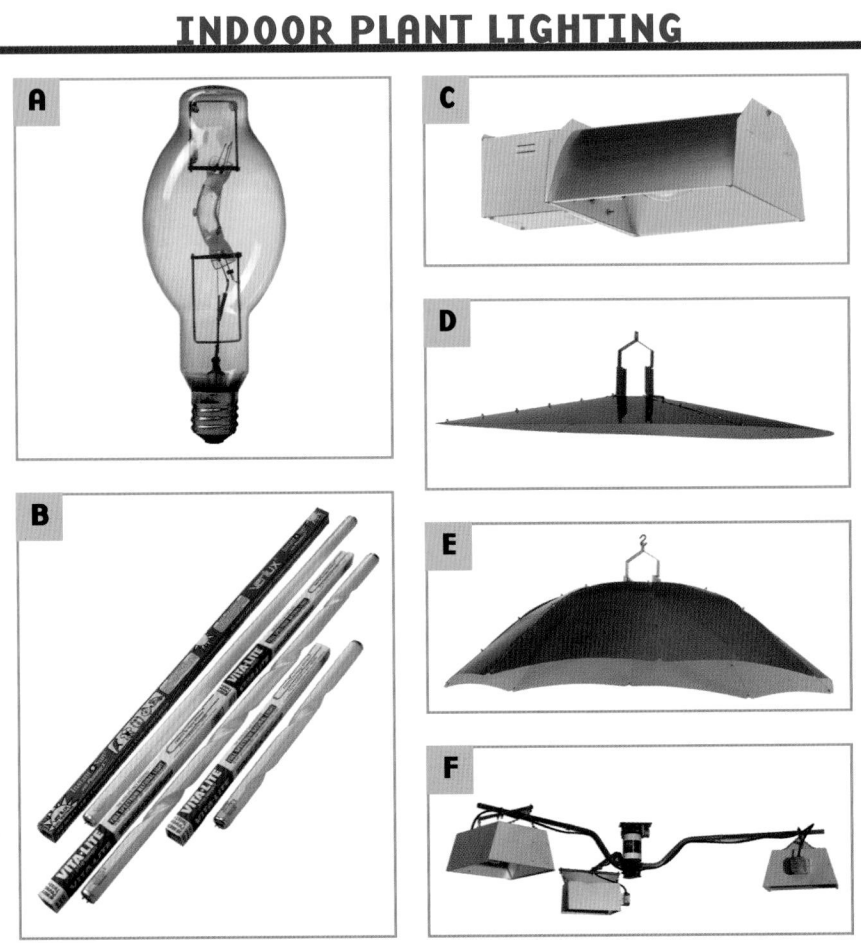

Equipment options for optimal illumination: metal halide (MH) bulbs (**A**) give off light that is most like natural sunlight. They fit into special fixtures (**C**). Full-spectrum bulbs (**B**) fit into standard 24- or 48-inch grow light fixtures. Reflectors (**D** and **E**) direct all available light toward the plants. Light movers (**F**) provide even light coverage.

Two additional pieces of equipment are important in your artificial light setup: a reflector and a light mover. Light movers are most important for growers who are concerned about even light coverage and who have experienced light burn on the upper foliage in their indoor garden. There are two basic types of light movers: linear and circular. Both are mounted on the ceiling above your growing area and keep the attached lights in constant motion above your plants.

Reflectors are an important consideration for everyone who gardens under artificial light. Most efficient are double parabolic reflectors, which direct all available light down toward the plants. A flat reflector is less efficient because it reflects some light back onto the bulbs. Unpainted aluminum can reflect light unevenly, resulting in hot spots that may burn foliage, so look for a reflector painted white.

While HID lamps are the first choice for serious interior landscapers, fluorescent lights are not completely obsolete. Improvements in grow bulbs and the affordability of bulbs and fixtures make fluorescents a popular option. Seeds can be started under regular cool or warm white bulbs, and some plants can be grown successfully under these less expensive, easy-to-find-lights. Full-spectrum fluorescent tubes (available in standard 24- and 48-inch lengths for grow-light fixtures) are a good option, promoting healthier plant growth while emitting a more pleasant light for the human inhabitants of your landscape.

As with HID lamps, it's best to use fluorescent lights with curved reflectors that direct maximum light toward the plants. However, there is an extra consideration with fluorescent tubes: they give off less light from the ends of the tubes than from the center. Place plants requiring lower light under the three inches of tube at either end of the fixture. Additionally, replace fluorescent tubes every 18 months if you use them approximately 16 hours per day.

Incandescent grow bulbs are the least efficient means of artificial illumination, since much of their energy is given off as heat, rather than as visible light. They have some merit, however. They emit an attractive white light and are a more than adequate light source for certain low-light foliage plants. Since these bulbs are hot, be sure not to place the foliage too close to the light, or it will burn.

The Agrosun Power Gro Bulb is a mercury vapor light with a broader spectrum and considerably more power than incandescent grow bulbs. It is a self-ballasted, 150-watt bulb that can be used in any floodlight-type lamp with a ceramic socket. Like the incandescent grow bulb, it gets hot, so be sure to place foliage at a safe distance from the fixture.

Whether you start out by supplementing existing light or by creating a garden with no natural light whatsoever, you will soon realize that artificial illumination allows you to push your interior landscaping envelope. Your only limits are your budget and your imagination.

GROWING TIPS

BIOLOGICAL PEST CONTROL IN THE INDOOR LANDSCAPE

SHILA PATEL

DESPITE THE UNIVERSAL IMPULSE to create Edenic plant-scapes in our homes, whether miniature groves of exotic palms, small-scale orangeries, or tiny lagoons filled with subtropical flora and fauna, we rarely envision or create a place for insects. But enlightened gardeners know that even small indoor plant collections require a balance of organisms for long-term health. For many interior landscapes, biological pest control can play an important role.

Successful control requires an integrated program of low-impact methods beginning with simple modifications in plantscape culture and mechanical controls such as traps, handpicking, and hosing. These need to be supplemented occasionally with the use of organic insecticides and biological pest controls like beneficial insects, such as lady beetles and green lacewings, and bacteria, such as *Bt* (*Bacillus thuringiensis*), to keep pest populations in check.

CULTURAL CONTROLS

Cultural controls—simple modifications in plant care—can have a significant impact on reducing or avoiding pest problems. These controls include adjusting the light, temperature, and humidity of the environment to best suit the types of plants in the collection in order to discourage pests and favor beneficial insects. Another cultural practice that can benefit indoor plants is reducing fertilizer nitrogen levels to the minimum amount required to maintain plant health and sustain slow growth. Excess nitrogen not only produces tender, succulent growth that is very susceptible to insect damage, but also triggers the reproductive cycles of insects like aphids, mealybugs, scales, and whiteflies. Slow-release or organic fertilizers, such as fish emulsion, which are low in nitrogen, are the best choices for interior landscapes.

Proper watering indoors is also important because excessive watering can encourage soilborne fungi and pests. Many indoor plants benefit from overhead watering and frequent misting, which increases humidity levels and prevents dust from accumulating on the foliage.

Other useful cultural controls, indoors as well as outdoors, include good sanitation (using clean soil, tools, pots, and promptly removing plant debris), regular pruning and pinching back to promote healthy growth, and removing and disposing of diseased or damaged plant tissue immediately.

PHYSICAL AND MECHANICAL CONTROLS

Like cultural controls, physical and mechanical controls should be incorporated into a program of daily plant care. The first and perhaps most important way to control pests is prevention: before purchasing any plants, examine them, checking the undersides of leaves and the roots, to ensure they are healthy and pest and disease free. Even if new plants appear to be healthy, set them aside in a quarantine area and monitor them for several weeks before introducing them into the plantscape.

A combination of cultural and mechanical methods is often sufficient to control low levels of infestation. Simply hosing off plants regularly with a strong jet of water may control soft-bodied insects like spider mites and aphids. Some pests, like whiteflies, can be vacuumed off plants early in the morning when they tend to be less active. Other simple controls include handpicking larger insects, rubbing off slow-moving clinging insects like mealybugs and scales, and wiping away egg cases and larvae. To control and monitor levels of aphids, whiteflies, and fungus gnats, place yellow, sticky-coated traps near plants. Similarly designed blue sticky traps are available for thrips. Neither trap attracts beneficial insects, and both can serve as good indicators of infestation levels.

LOW-IMPACT PESTICIDES

Although some pests quickly develop a resistance to pesticides, in situations where they cannot be controlled by cultural and mechanical methods, the judicious use of low-impact pesticides is the wisest course. These are ideal for reducing high pest populations before introducing beneficial insects into the indoor garden and to control occasional flare-ups.

GROWING TIPS

Low-impact pesticides, those with little or no residual effects, range from insecticidal soaps, pyrethrin, alcohol, horticultural oils, and combinations of these, to biological controls like *Bt*. Swabbing mealybugs and scales with rubbing alcohol, which destroys their protective coat, is sufficient to kill them. Some waxy-foliage plants can even tolerate a spray of rubbing alcohol mixed with water, but test a small section before spraying the whole plant.

INSECTICIDAL SOAP

Widely available, insecticidal soap is a combination of oils and an alkaline that penetrates certain insects' cuticle and damages cell membranes, killing insects on contact with no residual effects. Insecticidal soaps, which can also be made at home by combining a few tablespoons of household detergent with a gallon of warm water, are most effective against soft-bodied insects like aphids, mealybugs, scales, mites, and fungus gnats, but they will also kill beneficial insects. Spray soap on plants or use it as a soil drench to control fungus gnat larvae.

HORTICULTURAL OIL, NEEM, AND PYRETHRIN

To smother insects, use horticultural oil, typically a two-percent solution of refined petroleum oil in water. Use oils formulated for indoors to control insects such as aphids, mealybugs, mites, and young scales. Pyrethrin is a botanical pesticide derived from chrysanthemums (*Chrysanthemum cinerariaefolium*). It knocks down flying insects and kills many insects on contact, including aphids, mealybugs, whiteflies, armored scale, spider mites, and fungus gnats. It degrades quickly so can be used up to a week before introducing beneficial insects. Like pyrethrin, neem is a botanical pesticide, extracted from the seeds of the neem tree (*Azadirachta indica*). Neem affects insects' hormones, killing insects as they emerge from eggs or molt, and it is also a repellent.

BT

The most common biological pesticide is *Bt*, a type of bacteria. Unlike the other pesticides mentioned, it is host specific—different strains of the bacteria will control only certain pests, and only during specific stages of their life cycles. Because it is selective, it will not harm beneficial insects. Indoors, mix *Bt israelensis* or *Bt* H-14 with water and drench the soil where fungus gnats are a problem.

BENEFICIAL INSECTS INDOORS

Beneficial insects can be easily integrated into indoor pest management. Many beneficials are practically invisible or will remain near plants, where they feed. But some of the common ones, lady beetles and green lacewings, are visible; the adults are attracted to light, congregating near windows, and may leave specks (droppings) around the house. Before introducing beneficial insects indoors, review the checklist on this page.

GENERAL PREDATORS

GREEN LACEWINGS: At the larval stage, green lacewings (*Chysoperla carnea, C. rufilabris*) are voracious consumers of aphids. They also eat other soft-bodied insects including thrips, mealybugs, scales, and spider mites. Lacewings are typically sold as eggs or larvae. Eggs can be stored at room temperature for a few days. To distribute them, shake several on to the plant base or crotch, avoiding places where they might be washed away. Alternatively, place one to two larvae on each plant. When mature, lacewings feed only on nectar and pollen and should be fed an artificial diet, which causes egg-laying to increase dramatically.

LADY BEETLES AND CRYPTS: There are hundreds of species of lady beetles, but the convergent lady beetle (*Hippodamia convergens*) is the most common for indoor use. They are enthusiastic predators of aphids and will also consume whiteflies. Other lady beetle species feed on different insects including mealybugs, scale, thrips, and mites. Before releasing lady beetles, lightly mist plants. Release adults under plant stems at night or early in the morning, when temperatures are low and the beetles are less active. If possible, enclose adults with the plants in a net tent to prevent them from leaving. Adult crypts, also known as mealybug destroyers (*Cryptolaemus montrouzieri*), look like black lady beetles. As their name suggests, they feed on mealybugs and scales.

INSECTS: DO'S AND DON'TS

- Do not use residual pesticides for at least a month before introducing beneficials.
- Do not use pyrethrin or *Bt* for at least a week before introduction.
- Learn the basics of the pest's life cycle so that you can time the introduction to be most effective.
- Plan ahead, ordering beneficials at the first sign of pests, before the problem gets out of control.
- Contact an insectary, describe your specific problem, and choose the species best suited for your site.
- To give beneficials a head start, reduce the pest population first with low-impact pesticides.
- Provide food and water, and appropriate temperature and humidity levels for beneficials.
- Learn to distinguish between beneficial insects and pests.
- Monitor the situation, keeping a journal to determine your control program's effectiveness, and to predict future pest cycles.

GROWING TIPS

BENEFICIAL INSECTS

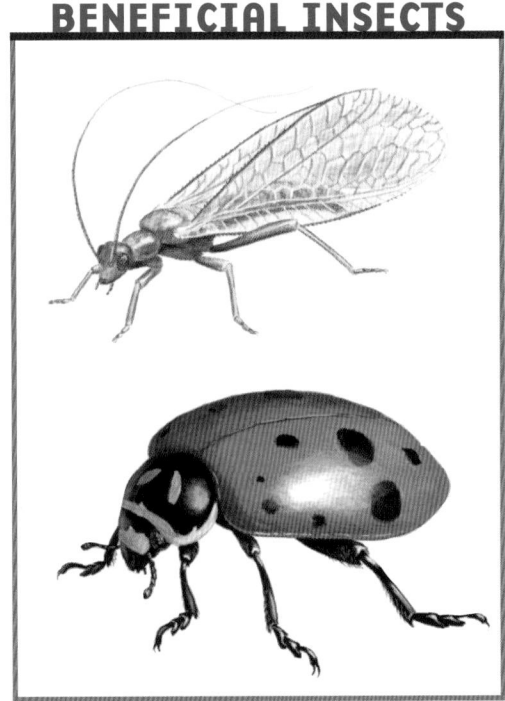

INDOOR PESTS AND THEIR PREDATORS

APHIDS

Aphids belong to the same order as mealybugs, scales, and whiteflies; all of them produce honeydew. Among the thousands of aphid species, some are very plant specific, but the green peach aphid (*Myzus persicae*) is most common indoors. Its predators include green lacewing, convergent lady beetle, and the aphid-eating gall midge (*Aphidoletes aphidimyza*), which looks like a tiny fly.

SPIDER MITES

Spider mites are the most common indoor pest mite and can be controlled by introducing predatory mites. Often smaller than their prey, these tiny arachnids feed on both eggs and adult spider mites and will not leave plants. Several species are available, most commonly *Amblyseius californicus*, *Metaseiulus occidentalis*, and *Phytoseiulus persimilis*; all prefer higher humidity than pest mites. For best results, release a combination of the beneficials. Sprinkle a few predators on each plant, depending on the severity of the problem.

MEALYBUGS

Mealybugs can rapidly develop insecticide-resistant populations, so are best controlled with crypts (*Cryptolaemus montrouzieri*). At the larval stage, this small beetle looks very similar to the mealybugs it feeds on. Use about five crypts per plant, distributing them in the early morning or late evening.

SCALES

Scales are closely related to mealybugs, despite their distinctive appearance. Both armored scales (Diaspidae), which carry viruses, and soft scales (Coccidae) are most vulnerable to soaps and oil when young, but beneficial insects are a good control for mature populations. These include parasitoids that lay their eggs in the scales and feed on them. Use the tiny yellow miniwasp (*Aphytis melinus*) for armored scales and the tiny black and yellow miniwasp (*Metaphycus helvolus*) for soft scales. Scale predators include crypts, which should be used in combination with green lacewings; the latter eat both young and mature scale in areas where crypts may not be able to reach them.

WHITEFLIES

Among the numerous species, greenhouse whitefly (*Trialeurodes vaporariorum*) is most common on indoor plants. For decades, the tiny yellow miniwasp (*Encarsia formosa*) has been an effective parasitoid, but it requires warmer (80° F.), more humid conditions (70 percent), and more light than many indoor environments can provide. Release about one to five wasps per plant, depending on the infestation. Insecticidal soap will kill the miniwasps.

Opposite: Indoor pest problems can often be tackled by introducing beneficial insects. Green lacewing, top, and convergent lady beetle are popular, as they feast on many pests that may plague your plants.

Right from top: Aphid, whitefly (adult and nymphs), mealybug, and scale are some of the pests that you may encounter in your indoor landscape.

Note: illustrations not to scale.

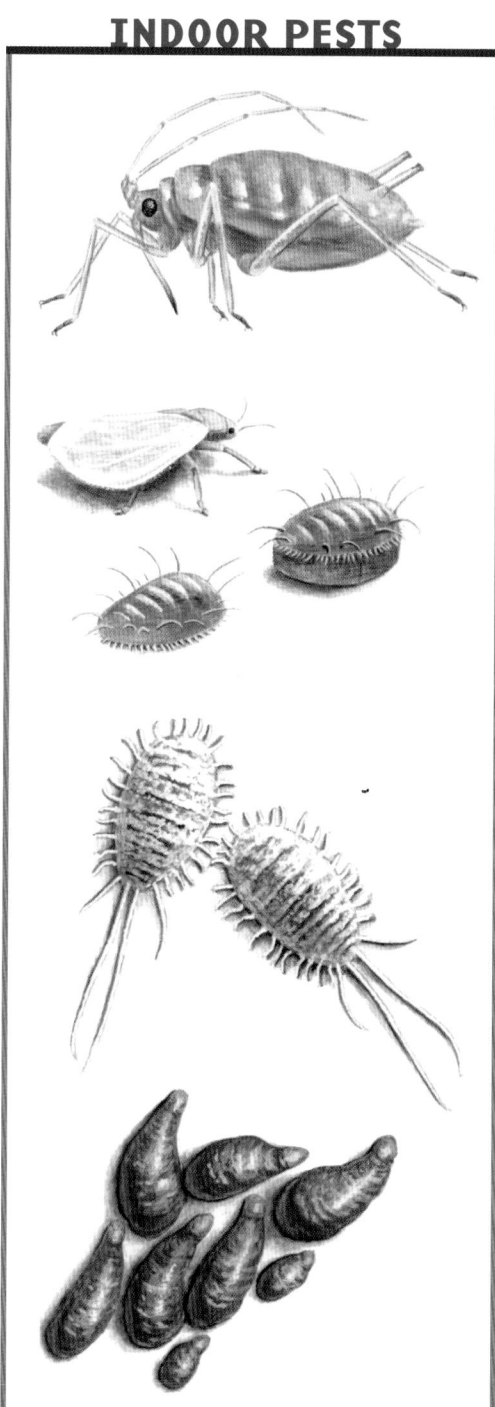

INDOOR PESTS

FOR MORE INFORMATION

THE COMPLETE GUIDE TO CONSERVATORY PLANTS
Ann Bonar. The Overlook Press, Woodstock, New York 1996

INDOOR BONSAI
Brooklyn Botanic Garden. *Plants & Gardens:* Vol. 46, No. 3 Fall 1990

A NEW LOOK AT HOUSEPLANTS
Brooklyn Botanic Garden: *Plants & Gardens* Vol. 49, No.4 Winter 1993

INDOOR GARDENING
Brooklyn Botanic Garden. *Plants & Gardens:* Vol. 43, No. 1 Fall 1987

FOLIAGE PLANTS FOR DECORATING INDOORS
Virginie F. & George A. Elbert
Timber Press, Portland Oregon, 1989

PLANTS THAT REALLY BLOOM INDOORS
Virginie F. & George A. Elbert
Simon and Schuster
New York 1974

INDOOR BONSAI
Paul Lesniewicz
Blandford Press
England, 1986

THE NEW HOUSEPLANT: BRINGING THE GARDEN INDOORS
Elvin McDonald. Macmillan Publishing Company, New York 1993

ONCE UPON A WINDOWSILL: A HISTORY OF INDOOR PLANTS
Tovah Martin, Timber Press. Portland, Oregon 1988

ARCHIVAL BOOKS

THE PARLOUR GARDENER: A PRACTICAL TREATISE ON THE HOUSE CULTIVATION OF ORNAMENTAL PLANTS
(Anonymous) Sampson, Low, Son & Co., London 1863

THE AMERICAN WOMAN'S HOME
Catherine E. Beecher & Harriet Beecher Stowe
J. B. Ford & Co, 1869

DOMESTIC FLORICULTURE
F. W. Burbidge, William Blackwood and Sons Edinburgh and London 1874

FLORAL DECORATIONS FOR DWELLING HOUSES
Annie Hassard
Macmillan & Co.
London, 1875

WINTER GREENERIES
Edwin A. D. Johnson
D. Orange Judd Company, New York, 1878

INDOOR PLANTS AND HOW TO GROW THEM
E. A. Maling. Smith, Elder and Co., London 1861

FLOWERS FOR THE PARLOR AND GARDEN
Edward Sprague Rand, Jr., Tilton & Co. Boston 1864

ON THE GROWTH OF PLANTS IN CLOSELY GLAZED CASES
Nathaniel B. Ward, John Van Voorst, Paternoster Row, London, 1852

SUPPLIERS

PLANTS FOR WARDIAN CASES

LOGEE'S GREENHOUSES
141 North Street
Danielson, CT 06239
888-330-8038

GLASSHOUSE WORKS
Church Street
P.O. Box 97
Stewart, OH 45778
740-662-2142
www.glasshouseworks.
com

WARDIAN CASES

TERRY HUGHES GLASS GARDENS
2027 Hillside Road
Fairfield, CT 06430
203-255-6549

H. POTTER
P.O. Box 6144
Lincoln, NE 68506
402-486-1455

TREES AND SHRUBS

THE BANANA TREE, INC.
715 Northampton Street
Easton, PA 18042
610-253-9589
www.banana-tree.com

MISCELLANEOUS INDOOR PLANTS

NATURE'S CURIOSITY SHOP
Vista, CA 21084
760-726-1488
(variegated foliage
plants)

TROPIFLORA
3530 Tallevast Road
Sarasota, FL 34243
800-613-7520
www.tropiflora.com

AQUATIC PLANTS AND SUPPLIES

S. SCHERER & SONS WATER GARDEN
104 Waterside Road
Northport, NY 11768
631-261-7432

LILYPONS WATER GARDENS
P.O. Box 10
Buckeystown
MD 21717-0010
800-999-5459
www.lilypons.com

WATERFORD GARDENS
74 East Allendale Road
Saddle River, NJ 07458
201-327-0721

www.waterford-
gardens.com

PALMS

GERRY'S JUNGLE
730 Stallsworth Road
McDonough, GA 30252
770-957-9099
www.neotropic.com

THE GREEN ESCAPE
10130 Northlake Blvd.
3214-PMB 200 West
Palm Beach, FL 33412
561-792-2405
www.thegreenescape.com

JUNGLE MUSIC
3233 Brant Street
San Diego, CA 92103
619-291-4605
www.junglemusic.net
(make appointment)

RHAPIS GARDENS
P.O. Box 287
Gregory, TX 78359
361-643-2061
www.rhapisgardens.com

SOUTH COAST PALMS
960 El Caminito
Fallbrook, CA 92028
760-723-1354
www.plantsigns.com/
palmlist.html

CITRUS TREES

EDIBLE LANDSCAPING
P.O. Box 77
Afton, VA 22920
800-524-4156
www.eat-it.com

JENÉ'S TROPICALS
6831 Central Avenue
St. Petersburg, FL 33710
727-344-1668
www.tropicalfruit.com

JUST FRUITS
30 St. Frances Street
Crawfordville, FL 32327
850-926-5644 (catalog $3)

LOUISIANA NURSERY
5853 Hwy. 182
Opelousas, LA 70570
337-948-3696

OREGON EXOTICS NURSERY
1065 Messenger Road
Grants Pass, OR 97527
541-846-7578
www.exoticfruit.com

WOODLANDERS
1128 Colleton Avenue
Aiken, SC 29801
803-648-7522
www.woodland@triplet.net

INDOOR LIGHTS

HYDROFARM
755 Southpoint Boulevard
Petaluma, CA 94954-1495
800-634-9990

LIGHT MANUFACTURING CO.
1634 S.E. Brooklyn Street
Portland, OR 97202
800-669-5483; www.litemanu.com

GARDEN INDOORS
208 Route 13
Bristol, PA 19007
800-227-4567

BIOLOGICAL PEST CONTROLS

CHARLEY'S GREENHOUSE SUPPLY
17979 State Route 536
Mount Vernon, WA 98273
800-322-4707
www.charleysgreenhouse.com

GARDENS ALIVE
5100 Schenley Place
Lawrenceberg, IN 47025
812-537-8651
www.gardens-alive.com

HARMONY FARM SUPPLY AND NURSERY
3244 Gravenstein Hwy. North
Sebastopol, CA 95472
707-823-9125
www.harmonyfarm.com

PLANET NATURAL
1612 Gold Avenue
Bozeman, MT 59715
800-289-6656
www.planetnatural.com

TEA HERB FARM
2332 Tea Road
Tea, MO 63091
573-437-3053

HORTICULTURAL SOCIETIES
(Inquire about local chapters and fee)

AMERICAN BAMBOO SOCIETY
750 Krumkill Road
Albany, NY 12203
www.bamboo.org/abs

AMERICAN BEGONIA SOCIETY
157 Monument Road
Rio Dell, CA 95562

AMERICAN GLOXINIA AND GESNERIAD SOCIETY
c/o Rebecca Gmucs
4 Kingswood Drive
Orangeburg, NY 10962

AMERICAN ORCHID SOCIETY
6000 South Olive Avenue
West Palm Beach, FL 33405
www.orchidweb.org

ANYTHING BUT GREEN
(A society dedicated to plants with
colored or variegated foliage)
c/o Denis Garrett
P.O. Box 188
Pegram, TN 37143

BROMELIAD SOCIETY
c/o Carolyn Schoenau
P.O. Box 12981
Gainsville, FL 32604-0981
bsi@nersp.nerdc.ufl.edu

INDOOR GARDENING SOCIETY OF AMERICA
c/o Sharon Zentz
944 South Munroe Road
Tallmadge, OH 44278

INTERNATIONAL AROID SOCIETY
P.O. Box 43-1853
Miami, FL 33143

SOUTHEASTERN PALM AND EXOTIC PLANT SOCIETY
c/o Tom McClendon
4531 Highway 15 South
Greensboro, GA 30642

TERRARIUM ASSOCIATION
P.O. Box 276
Newfane, VT 05345
802-824-3126
(No memberships)

ANTIQUE BOOK DEALERS

ELISABETH WOODBURN, BOOKS
P.O. Box 398
Hopewell, NJ 08525
609-466-0522
woodburn@prodigy.net

LARRY W. PRICE BOOKS
353 N. W. Maywood Drive
Portland, OR 97210-3333
503-221-1410
www.abebooks.com

RAYMOND M. SUTTON, JR.
P.O. Box 330
Williamsburg, KY 40769
606-549-3464
www.suttonbooks.com

HINCK & WALL
P.O. Box 32266
1820 35th Street NW
Washington D.C. 20007
202-965-3785
hinckandwall@mindspring.com

CONTRIBUTORS

SCOTT D. APPELL is director of education for the Horticultural Society of New York and a member of the Publications Committee of the Pennsylvania Horticultural Society. He is a contributing author to Smith & Hawken's *Book of Outdoor Gardening* and Rodale Press' *1001 Ingenious Gardening Ideas* as well as a botanical consultant for *Gardens by the Sea: Creating a Tropical Paradise*, published by the Garden Club of Palm Beach. In addition, he has written three books, *Pansies,Tulips*, and *Lilies*, all published by Friedman/Fairfax Publishers, Inc, New York. His private consultation company is called The Green Man.

SUSANNE LUCAS is a free-lance horticultural consultant, garden designer, and landscape gardener. Among the many plants she has encountered, it is her passion for bamboos that has endured. Over ten years ago she set out to grow only the cold-hardiest bamboos in her garden in coastal Massachusetts and continues searching the globe for those still not in cultivation. She is president of the American Bamboo Society.

TOM McCLENDON is president of the Southeastern Palm and Exotic Plant Society and an avid grower of palms, citrus, and other subtropical plants. He has given numerous talks across the country and is the author of several articles on these subjects. He is also the co-author of *The Palm Reader*, a book on the outdoor cultivation of palms in the South (in press). In his day job, Tom is an assistant principal in Augusta, Georgia, where he lives with his wife Kay and their two children, Jacob and Daniel.

SHILA PATEL is the garden web editor at Martha Stewart Living Omnimedia and the former managing editor of *National Gardening* magazine.

BILL SHANK was the cofounder (in 1984), and first president of the Horticultural Alliance of the Hamptons, in Bridgehampton, New York. He is currently vice-president/deputy garden editor of Martha Stewart Living Omnimedia. In addition, he serves both on the Garden Committee of Wave Hill and the Board of the Metro-Hort Group, based in New York City. He co-designed and maintained a much-publicized garden on eastern Long Island from 1981 until 1995. He presently lives and gardens indoors in New York City.

JULIA SOLARZ is the editor of *DIG*, an award-winning bimonthly gardening magazine, published by the nursery Hortus in Pasadena, California. She grows potted cacti and succulents year-round in the courtyard of her Spanish-style, Hollywood Hills home, where the mild climate allows for such a luxury.

MOBEE WEINSTEIN is assistant foreman of gardeners at the New York Botanical Garden, where she has worked for the past 20 years. She is a graduate of the NYBG School of Horticulture and received a Bachelor's Degree in Plant Studies. Her primary work is with ferns, tropical, and aquatic plants and she is a past president of the New York Chapter of the American Fern Society. She is an instructor for the NYBG School of Professional Horticulture and Continuing Education Department, is an Adjunct Professor for SUNY at Farmingdale and lectures frequently.

ELLEN ZACHOS is a Harvard graduate and received her Certificate in Horticulture from The New York Botanical Garden. She specializes in tropical plants and has restored several greenhouses in the New York City area, which she now maintains for her clients. Her company, ACME Plant Stuff, installs and maintains commercial and residential interior and exterior gardens in New York City.

ILLUSTRATIONS AND PHOTOS

Four Indoor Garden Designs by **BILL SHANK**
All critters by **STEVE BUCHANAN**
Archival material courtesy of **SCOTT D. APPELL**
VICTOR SCHRAGER cover, pages 5, 21, 30
DAVID CAVAGNARO pages 1, 23 bottom left, 35 bottom left and right, 49, 50, 53, 58, 61, 62, 64, 73, 76
ALAN & LINDA DETRICK pages 6, 23 top left and right, bottom right, 35 top left and right, 39, 40, 45, 67, 74, 75 top, 77, 79, 87 top and bottom, 90
JUDY WHITE/GARDENPHOTOS.COM pages 11, 59, 70, 75 bottom
ELLEN ZACHOS pages 25, 28, 29 left and right, 88, 89
JOE LeVERT page 41
FLORA GRAPHICS pages 37, 38
SUSANNE LUCAS pages 43, 44, 47
WILLIAM H. ALLEN, JR. page 52
ROY JANSEN (Jasmine Blue, Sherman Oaks, CA) page 54
BRAD SMITH (Red Desert, San Francisco, CA) pages 56 top and bottom, 57 top and bottom
ELVIN McDONALD page 66
MOBEE WEINSTEIN pages 68, 71
SUNLIGHT SUPPLY, INC. page 91
LIGHT MANUFACTURING CO. page 94 all

INDEX

BROOKLYN BOTANIC GARDEN

MORE

BOOKS ON

GARDENING

INDOORS